RADIO—
The Forgotten Medium

RADIO—
The Forgotten Medium

Edward C. Pease
Everette E. Dennis

Editors

Transaction Publishers
New Brunswick (U.S.A.) and London (U.K.)

This book is printed on acid-free paper that meets the American National Standard for Permanence of Paper for Printed Library Materials.

Library of Congress Catalog Number: 94-32128
ISBN: 1-56000-798-2
Printed in the United States of America

Library of Congress Cataloging-in-Publication Data

Radio—the forgotten medium / edited by Edward C. Pease and Everette E. Dennis.
    p. cm.
Originally published in the Media studies journal, summer 1993.
Includes bibliographical references (p. -) and index.
ISBN 1-56000-798-2 (acid-free)
    1. Radio broadcasting—Social aspects. 2. Radio broadcasting—History.
I. Pease, Edward C. II. Dennis, Everette E. III. Media studies journal.
PN1991.6.R24   1994
302.23'44—dc20   94-32128
                                               CIP

Contents

"Once the marvel of the age, the glue that held a nation together through war and economic depression, radio is now perceived as occupying a corner chair at media family gatherings—a maiden aunt, beloved but past her prime. Not so," contends the author, a Boston College professor, offering a context for the oldest broadcast medium, then and now. Radio is as vital today as it was 50 years ago.

If nothing else, radio has proven itself able to adapt, Phoenix-like, to whatever comes—television, format wars, contests and worse, argues the publisher of *Radio Ink* magazine. So satellites, digital broadcasting and other new technologies don't mean a thing—challenges have always meant opportunity for radio.

"The history of radio is suffused with politics," observes a political scientist at Barnard College. Similarly, political history is suffused with radio. From the 1920 Harding-Cox presidential returns on Pittsburg's KDKA to the Clinton-Bush-Perot fight in 1992, radio has been at the center of American politics—"the people's university."

When the *Titanic* sank in 1912, radio was there. And that role—providing information in times of trouble—is still just one of the things that radio does best, observes the president of the Radio-Television News Directors Association. "When hurricanes hit, when traffic is snarled, when the World Trade Towers are bombed, when the Orioles are in town—give radio 22 minutes (or less) and get the world."

Part II Radio as Cultural Expression

The 1990s may seem to have heralded the Age of Talk Radio Democracy, but that noise over the airwaves doesn't necessarily reflect America, contend researchers at the Times Mirror Center for the People & the Press, based on their national survey. "Rather than genuinely reflect widespread public disquiet, the voices of the vocal minority caricature and exaggerate discontent," they conclude.

Some say talk shows are the expression of democracy in the 1990s. "But irksome questions remain," muses a radio historian. "Is our 'Doctor of Democracy' really serving us? Is it a victory for electronic democracy, or is this glut of hot air more along the lines of Pyrrhus' sentiment: 'Another victory like that and we're done for'?"

"Americans used to be able to talk over the backyard fence," observes a Washington, D.C., talk show host. "Now, talk shows have expanded the nation's back yard." Talk radio makes an important contribution to the social discourse, she says, one essential to the functioning of democracy.

If you are what you eat, so are you what you hear, suggests the author, a longtime radio connoisseur. "Just as our physical bodies are the sum of the meals we have eaten, our minds are a sum of what we have heard, read and thought." Tasty stuff, radio.

America's airwaves reflect all the idiosyncracies, diversity, qualities and quirkiness of a nation. This sampling of eight of its 11,338 stations from across the country—country, sports, Christian, rock and more—are a sound snapshot of the customs, values and foibles of radio in America 1993.

"If music radio were truly fragmented, Miami would still have an easy-listening station, Seattle would still have commercial jazz, and Detroit would still have R&B oldies," writes the author, a record industry executive and longtime radio observer in a critical tour of the radio music scene.

"In the broadcasting marketplace, as in other jungles, it comes down to survival of the fittest," contends a broadcasting scholar. "AM radio is not exactly a finely tuned athlete—either in technological or programming terms—so its slow fade may simply be Darwinism at work."

Part III   The Global Airwaves

Anglo-American self-absorption aside, 95 percent of the world's radio listeners are not American or British, observes a French media scholar—they reside in nations where radio is a central part of daily life. "What is too often forgotten about radio is that part of it that operates outside Britain and the United States," he adds.

The onslaught of television in the 1950s had backed radio against a wall and the BBC found it necessary to argue for the "maiden aunt of broadcasting." Today, observes the leading historian of British broadcasting, people are "panting" to start up radio stations in Britain.

In case there was any question of the importance of BBC's Radio 4 in England's daily life, response to a plan to shift schedules was answer enough, thank you very much. "The British public had its knickers in a twist," recalls a BBC producer. "The calming inevitability of Life As We Know It was under attack."

For decades, as East and West eyed one another over the Iron Curtain, one weapon in the struggle was radio. "Ironically, the easing of Cold War tensions and the spread of democracy have not meant fewer clandestine radio operations but more," a scholar of international radio observes. There may be more struggles now, not fewer.

Part IV The Structure of Radio

Serving local interests and diversity in a tightening radio marketplace is the challenge facing both radio and those charged with its regulation, explains an FCC commissioner. In the face of new political, economic and technological imperatives, regulators committed to localism and diversity have their work cut out for them.

New technology may alter how radio functions, but it won't alter one immutable fact about the industry, argues an officer of the National Association of Broadcasters. "In no other media business do competitors expend proportionately so much time, effort and money to so thoroughly research and strategize over the audience's psyche."

"For most financial analysts, the days when the radio industry stood center stage have long passed," writes a media analyst and investment banker. "Few have anything more than oral history to generate even the vaguest images of radio's preeminence in the media field."

The creation of the Corporation for Public Broadcasting in 1967 meant that 86 percent of the U.S. population could tune in public radio. Even today, argues a longtime public radio professional, "people want more from radio than top 40, Limbaugh, the same news and endless ads. That's where America—and public radio—live."

In the early 1970s, a man from Buffalo had a wacky idea—a 90-minute radio news magazine he called "All Things Considered." Two decades later, National Public Radio draws 10 million listeners a week, points out NPR's vice president for news and information. "The size of NPR's audience and the kind of people who listen challenge old assumptions that public radio is just for 'zither concert' types," he says.

In the 10 years since American Public Radio was born, the system has become a premier distributor of programming for public radio stations. The president of APR (now known as Public Radio International) describes how competition has enriched the public radio marketplace.

Part V Books

From comedy to jukeboxes, drama to war coverage, politics to social commentary, radio has been central to American life in this century, observes a broadcast historian, in reviewing seven books on radio. It's time to recognize radio's role, "a dependable companion and friend," she writes. "To overlook radio is to miss the big picture."

Preface

At a time when the eyes of many in the world who care about media are fixed on the information superhighway—an enterprise that potentially connects all available information, entertainment and messaging to a global audience of billions—radio may seem like a technology whose time has come and gone. At best, many may view radio affectionately, like a lingering great aunt, now pushed to the periphery. Surely, such observers argue, radio was outdistanced decades ago by television, later by cable and now by new interactive media, data streams and so much more.

Like the air, radio is just there, part of the media and social landscape but rarely acknowledged or much remarked. At least, that is one image of radio, once a dominant force in the world's media life but now "the forgotten medium," no longer as glamorous or important as its shinier successors.

In response to such talk comes author and humorist Garrison Keillor, perhaps radio's staunchest champion: "Radio isn't forgotten by its legions of listeners, only by people who don't listen, and who cares about them?" he retorts. "I am always being asked by newspaper editors if I think that radio has a future or can make a comeback—some idiot question like that—and it's tiresome to try to respond, as if one were asked to defend the existence of trees." In his 30s, Keillor rediscovered radio, a favorite companion of his youth, and created the popular program "Prairie Home Companion," distributed weekly by American Public Radio, that serves as a kind of metaphor for radio's resilience and vitality.

Radio, of course, is not forgotten at all by the billions around the globe who depend on it daily. In some places, such as China and Indonesia, it is the most pervasive of all media. Elsewhere, as in the United States, it may be a secondary medium but remains truly ubiquitous. As the first broadcast medium, radio created formats and structures that television later adopted. But it did much more by demonstrating its versatility, moving from one format to another and reversing the role of entertainment and information while still holding onto advertising dollars and revving up anew its capacity as opinion maker.

To those who thought radio was on a downhill slope just a few years ago, the runaway success of talk show hosts like Larry King, Howard Stern, Rush Limbaugh and others is proof positive that the decline was short-lived. Drawing massive audiences and luring advertisers, these talkmeisters have considerable impact on public opinion. Indeed, during the 1992 presidential campaign, when people spoke of the new "electronic democracy" they were referring largely to radio talk shows, as well as to TV talk and variety shows and MTV. Just because critics and media scholars don't attend much to radio (and they don't) does not mean that the medium is unimportant. When the president of the United States, whether Ronald Reagan or Bill Clinton, does a weekly radio broadcast, you can be sure it isn't just to mark time. There's good evidence, in fact, that people who may not generally pay much attention to announcements on television or in the press do catch them on the radio while driving to and from work, while working or relaxing.

While this volume mostly emphasizes the state of radio in the United States, it also includes four essays touching on the medium's massive global impact as well. Surely no one—entrepreneurs, politicians or least of all the public—is counting radio out. Radio is, as they say, here to stay, more vital than ever even while conceding center stage to its flashier cousin, television, and their even hipper new interactive relatives sprouting up along the information highway. Despite these new arrivals, radio remains the most pervasive medium worldwide. Television is hot on its heels even in developing countries, but that does not mean that radio won't continue to prosper much as it continues to do in the United States and in other information societies where its role is constantly refined and fragmented, but remains vitally important. The old radio networks may be largely gone, but the cumulative effect of radio as carrier of music, news and disaster information is immense.

Neither is radio to be counted out on the information highway. Delano Lewis, president of National Public Radio who came to his post in 1993 from the field of telecommunications, vows that radio will have an important place in the new, linked electronic world. And it already does, in fact, using satellites to extend its signal reach far beyond local stations, with storage capacity that permits rebroadcast later. When all the tools and vehicles available for the information superhighway are seriously considered, radio will still have its special place, recognized as a force-ful, cost-effective member of the media family.

This volume originally was issued as the Summer 1993 issue of the *Media Studies Journal*, published by The Freedom Forum Media Studies Center at Columbia University in New York City. It has since been modified, reedited and augmented by the editors for a larger audience. The editors are especially grateful to Lisa DeLisle for her assistance in editing, repositioning and moving the manuscript to completion. And, as always, we are in the debt of Irving Louis Horowitz for his leadership at Transaction Publishers which made this book possible.

It is our hope that this book will be of value to students of media, communication, politics and society, as well as to anyone who cares about effective communication in this increasingly global society. To many, radio may be too familiar to be much noticed—"electronic wall-paper"—but it certainly is too widespread to be a forgotten medium.

> Everette E. Dennis
> Executive Director
> The Freedom Forum Media Studies Center
> Columbia University
> New York City
> February 1994

Introduction
Radio—The Forgotten Medium

Ask about "the media," and people think first of television, then newspapers. Sometimes, though not always, they acknowledge the existence of radio. It is not uncommon for media critics to ignore radio altogether in their treatment of the larger modern media mix. Although the average American owns multiple radios and lives with this most portable medium in every room in the house, in the office, the car and even in parks, mountain retreats and on the beach, radio is very rarely the topic of public discussion, giving it the dubious identity as "the forgotten medium." This, the oldest of the broadcast media and once the king of electronic media, has been pushed farther and farther into the background of the media family photo. Occasionally there are references in the press to a radio station sale, a new radio network or a controversy first ignited on radio, but such sightings of radio in the public discourse are cameo appearances at best, like those of a once-famous leading actor reduced to walk-on or character roles. But in truth, radio is much more than a bit player or aging "maiden aunt," as more than one author in this volume suggest.

A close look at radio demonstrates its vitality, its economic, political and social importance, as well as its staying power in the communication field. A recent flurry of articles about congressional hand-wringing over violence on the air and the Federal Communications Commission's concern about broadcasting for children demonstrated how far the radio star had fallen and how invisible the medium had become. In article after article, "broadcasting" meant only television—not radio. Radio program listings, once a staple of American newspapers, have virtually disappeared, save for a few agate-sized mentions, typically about talk shows. Once celebrated for its profound and highly visible role in popular culture, radio has for years now taken a seat far from center stage, seemingly in the shadows of the communications industry. In fact, aside from a handful of specialized trade publications, *Radio Times*, the popular monthly published by the BBC, may be the only mainstream magazine in the world that still honors radio with top billing.

Even New York's Museum of Broadcasting relegated the world's first broadcast medium to the background when it changed its name in 1991 to the Museum of Television and Radio. This prompted radio entertainer Garrison Keillor to implore his favorite medium to "work a little harder, struggle a little more" to receive its due, a notion that brought a smile to the face of the man who has championed the rights of shy people—as well as those of what has become a shy medium, pushed out of its once preeminent position by its younger and now dominant sibling, television.

All that said, no one should be deceived into thinking that radio is not alive and well or that it is no longer important on the world stage. Though snubbed by media coverage in the United States, radio remains the world's most ubiquitous medium, certainly the one with the widest reach and greatest penetration. The ease with which radio leaps national boundaries and its potential power for shaping public opinion are not lost on those who watched the fall of communism, first in Eastern Europe and then in the Soviet Union. In 1993, in a venue unrelated to radio, Polish President Lech Walesa told a Freedom Forum audience that what finally cracked the Iron Curtain was free media and "the need for objective information.... Especially radio," he said, which "brought information prohibited in our country. It raised our spirits, strengthened faith and hope. It created a feeling of togetherness and international solidarity of free people." Similarly, on the other side of the globe, the same could be said of the role of Radio Veritas in the Philippines, which helped solidify opposition to Ferdinand Marcos. And there are many examples in other countries where radio remains profoundly important, even in the age of television.

Radio in the United States garners a fraction (6.7 percent) of media advertising expenditures, which totaled $125.4 billion nationwide a year in the early 1990s. In comparison, newspapers got 24.1 percent of ad revenues, television 21.7 percent, direct mail 19.3 percent and 28.2 percent went to all other media. Most media suffered in the early 1990s, with overall ad spending down 1.7 percent nationally from 1990-91: Daily newspapers lost 5.8 percent, magazines 4.1 percent and television 3.5 percent (though cable advertising was up a whopping 15.2 percent); radio, while also losing, declined less than the others for the period, 2.9

percent. Rebounding somewhat since 1991, national radio ad revenues are expected to grow at an annual rate of 6.4 percent, to $11.5 billion by 1996, predicts the communications industry forecasting firm, Veronis, Suhler and Associates; television is expected to grow at 6.8 percent, to $32.8 billion by 1996, and newspapers by 6.7 percent to $59.8 billion. Even in times of economic recession, it is important to note, money spent on radio buys a lot. It is the least expensive and most targeted medium in which to "publish," and new satellite links and various programming networks ensure that radio will remain a vital force in communicating throughout American society and the world.

The influence of radio far exceeds its relative economic weight in the media market. National Public Radio, for example, is a major presence in the American news media, with clout far beyond what total audience numbers might indicate because of the upscale nature of its listeners. Ronald Reagan (whose communications savvy few question) brought back the presidential radio address, not as a nostalgic nod to Franklin Delano Roosevelt but because radio is a means of reaching millions of Americans not eager to sit passively in front of a television set. Bill Clinton continues that strategy, with White House staffers calling radio the easiest and most effective electronic means of getting the president's word out. This most portable electronic medium also is essential for anyone interested in instant news or popular music. It is still the most immediate and relied-upon emergency medium during times of disaster, with a reach broader than that of television, still serving distant and rural locations that have little or no local television service.

Radio's cultural function is probably best illustrated by the popularity of Garrison Keillor, whose "Prairie Home Companion"—originally a local program on Minnesota Public Radio before going national—makes creative demands on the senses, encouraging listeners to see, smell and feel Keillor's imaginary hometown of Lake Wobegon, "where all the women are strong, all the men are good looking and all the children are above average." In anyone's radio hall of fame, Keillor has first-rank inclusion, so strong is his influence on the character of the medium and its content. In his 1991 ode to radio, *WLT: A Radio Romance*, Keillor described the medium's impact on individuals. "Radio leaped the miles and came into every home with a bounty of cheerful information—what a boon!" Keillor wrote. "Radio was the remedy for isolation, which was the curse of the farmer. Now he had a friendly neighbor to sit down with at any hour of the day and tell him interest-ing things." More or less alone on the radio drama stage of the 1990s, Garrison Keillor does today what radio did in the 1930s and 1940s, during the medium's so-called golden age.

Social analysts have spent little time in recent years considering radio's changing functions after its initial metamorphosis upon the advent of tele-vision. Except for passing references to radio listeners' perceptions that Richard Nixon had won the famed 1960 presidential debates, while TV viewers thought he'd lost badly, not many scholars pay much attention to radio, its reach, impact and influence on life generally and within the media family more specifically. By the same token, with some notable excep-tions, media reporters and critics also have largely forgotten about radio.

It got some attention in the 1980s, when a resurgence of talk radio, for the most part hosted by conservative talkmeisters, was credited with the defeat of a congressional pay raise. Similarly, during the 1992 presi-dential campaign, the rise of Rush Limbaugh—the "Doctor of Democ-racy"—and the continued influence of Larry King reinforced the serious role of radio in American communication. Indeed, a study of the media and campaign '92 by The Freedom Forum Media Studies Center found that King, in his radio and television roles, was the second most-fre-quently cited pundit in press coverage of the presidential campaign, be-hind David Brinkley, doubtless a byproduct of independent candidate Ross Perot's patronage. Less often talked about these days but still a powerful radio force is the commentator Paul Harvey, who was deemed one of the most influential Americans of all time in a 1989 article in the *Media Studies Journal* by Frank Mankiewicz. In an essay titled "From Lippmann to Letterman: The 10 Most Powerful Voices," the eminent political adviser and communications specialist noted that in lists of the 10 most influential opinion-shapers of each decade since the 1930s, Paul Harvey's name appears most often, on five of the six lists. Harvey's durability and that of radio are worthy of much more consideration than they have gotten in recent years.

Radio's resilient nature points up the fact that a medium's place in the media family can change without signaling its death. There may be a message here for television as futurists ponder whether 500-channel cable systems will transform television into a medium as fragmented as its older sibling, radio. Books, newspapers and radio, all once confidently marked for extinction by one critic or another, not only live on but have new and refined missions in the world of modern communication.

With this volume, we and our authors affirm that radio is not only still with us, but remains a medium of great power and importance. Although television is closing in, radio still has greater reach and impact worldwide. On the domestic scene, the medium's changing role in a volatile and ever-shifting U.S. media market may have obscured its vitality and importance, something we hope will be reversed in the minds of critics, analysts, scholars and, most importantly, the public. Every indication we see—economic, demographic, social and democratic—suggests that, far from fading into the ether, radio is moving back into our consciousness and back into the mainstream. With any luck, the notion of radio as a forgotten medium will itself be soon forgotten.

In the introductory section of *Radio—The Forgotten Medium*, four authors combine to remind us of radio's social context, past, present and future. In her essay, "Resilient Radio," telecommunications scholar Marilyn J. Matelski of Boston College recalls radio's glory days and argues that the glory is not all past. Gazing in the opposite direction, B. Eric Rhoads, publisher of *Radio Ink* magazine, illustrates in "Looking Back at Radio's Future" how and why this is so. Satellites, digital broadcasting and other new technology aren't threats, he says, just new opportunities for radio. One of the first of those opportunities was politics, suggests Barnard College political scientist Michael X. Delli Carpini in "Radio's Political Past." Another, of course, is breaking news, as David Bartlett, president of the Radio-Television News Directors Association, reminds us in "News Radio—More Than Masters of Disaster."

With these perspectives as prologue, we move into a tour of radio formats with a collection of seven essays that look at "Radio as Cultural Expression." Leading this section are three pieces examining what is surely the hottest thing on radio in the 1990s—talk. From their national survey at the Times Mirror Center for the People & the Press, Andrew Kohut and Carol Bowman describe characteristics of "The Vocal Minority in U.S. Politics." Then, radio historian, educator and author Tom Lewis takes on a heavyweight of the air in "Triumph of the Idol—Rush Limbaugh and a Hot Medium," and Washington, D.C., talk show host Diane Rehm offers a less jaded perspective in "Talking Over America's Electronic Backyard Fence."

From talk to rock to news, the airwaves are a smorgasbord for the ear and the mind, suggests longtime radio connoisseur Adam Clayton Powell III, now director for technology studies at The Freedom Forum Media Studies Center, in "You Are What You Hear." In case there was any question of that, "Ear on America" offers a sampling of on-air tidbits from eight stations across the country as Al Stavitsky, a communications professor at the University of Oregon, provides a tour from Alaskan bush radio to all-sports in New York to contemporary Christian sounds in Waco, Texas, illustrating the industry's diversity, idiosyncrasies, quality and quirkiness. Of course, radio's staple is music, as Sean Ross, a record company executive and longtime radio writer, examines in "Music Radio—The Fickleness of Fragmentation." For many, growing up with radio meant that constant companion, the portable AM transistor. Once the giant of the airwaves, AM radio today is a sickly shadow of its former self, observes Boston College broadcast historian Michael C. Keith in "Whither (Or Wither?) AM?"

From the straits of AM, the next section, "Airwaves Abroad," offers a glimpse of the powerful position of radio around the world. The global tour begins with a look at "Radio Beyond the Anglo-American World" by Claude-Jean Bertrand, a media scholar at l'Université de Paris-2. Then, for an authoritative look at what is arguably the world's standard for radio, the BBC, we turn to Lord Asa Briggs, the world's preeminent broadcasting historian, for the word on "The BBC—From Maiden Aunt to Sexy Upstart." As one illustration of the central importance of the BBC to British life, Suzanne Levy, a BBC producer and Center research fellow, describes why her countrymen are "Devoted to Auntie Beeb." And finally, Marquette University broadcasting scholar Lawrence Soley concludes this section with a report on "Heating Up Clandestine Radio After the Cold War."

From formats and programming, we move to an examination of "The Structures of Radio"—economic, regulatory, social and technological—with six essays by authors intimately familiar with their assignments. Federal Communications Commissioner Andrew C. Barrett opens with a primer on regulation and radio in "Public Policy and Radio—A Regulator's View." Much of public policy in communications is technology-driven, says Richard V. Ducey of the National Association of Broadcasters as he goes "Riding Radio's Technological Wave" into a brave new electronic world. But financial markets are far from bullish on radio as a communications investment, observes Richard J. MacDonald, an investment banker and media financial analyst in "On the Business Side, an End to Radio Romance." MacDonald says bankers have tuned radio out. Three essays on the role and promise of public broadcasting wind up this section. Although just 1,592 of the nation's 11,338 radio stations are noncommercial, public radio's future is assured by the high quality of its programming and the dedication of its audience, the authors argue. First, longtime public radio professional Anna Kosof traces the history of public broadcasting in "Public Radio—Americans Want More," arguing that by failing to serve audiences, commercial radio creates niches for progressive and alternative public stations. In "Growing NPR," William E. Buzenberg, vice president for news and information at National Public Radio, describes how one of those niches has grown to accommodate 10 million listeners a week. And Steven L. Salyer, president of Minnesota-based American Public Radio (which in 1994 broadened its mission and changed its name to Public Radio International), celebrates the 10th anniversary of "the other" public radio system in "From Monopoly to Marketplace—Public Radio Comes of Age."

This volume concludes with a review of seven key books on radio that is really a *tour de force* of the industry—its history, its richness and diversity, its potential. In "Seems Radio Is Here to Stay," telecommunications Professor Mary Ann Watson of Eastern Michigan University suggests that "to overlook radio is to miss the big picture."

Our objective in drawing the collective wisdom of our 22 knowledgeable authors into a primer on the past, present and future of radio was to dispell the notion that television and, in turn, its interactive telecommunications cousins have closed the door on radio. As these essays clearly illustrate, radio is far from forgotten. Those who work in, study and love the medium apparently feel themselves a bit neglected, however, if response to the issue of *Media Studies Journal* from which this book is drawn was any indication. When it was released in summer 1993, more than 1,100 requests for copies poured in from new readers at radio stations, media companies, schools and universities worldwide. We hope that with this expanded volume we can further reassure radio aficionados that neither they nor their medium are forgotten. The editors would like to acknowledge the conbributions of *Media Studies Journal* assistant editor Lisa DeLisle in preparing this manuscript.

The Editors

I

Overview

SOME RADIO MILESTONES

1860 Scottish physicist James Clerk Maxwell hypothesizes the existence of radio waves

1887 German scientist Heinrich Hertz demonstrates existence of radio waves

1895 Guglielmo Marconi sends coded messages over radio waves at his father's Italian estate, obtains British patent for "wireless telegraph" in 1897

1901 Marconi's first trans-Atlantic radio message

1906 Reginald Fessenden broadcasts from Boston to ships at sea

1906 Lee DeForest develops the audion vacuum tube, which amplifies radio signals (puts Enrico Caruso on the air in 1910)

1912 Shore-side wireless operators (including David Sarnoff) pick up signals from the *S.S. Titanic*

1912 The Radio Act of 1912, the first U.S. law to regulate land radio stations, makes the secretary of Commerce and Labor responsible for licensing

1916 David Sarnoff outlines his plan to make the "radio music box" a "household utility"

1920 Westinghouse engineer Frank Conrad builds station 8XK in his garage in Pittsburgh; its successor, KDKA (now oldest existing station), goes on the air with 1920 presidential election returns

1922 First broadcast advertisement, over AT&T's WEAF in New York

1926 NBC, an RCA subsidiary, starts first permanent network with 24 stations; its first national broadcast, a 1927 football game. CBS radio network formed in 1927

1927 The Radio Act of 1927 establishes that the radio spectrum belongs to the people, and so should be regulated in the public interest. Federal Radio Commission is formed

1930 The half-million radio sets in use in the early 1920s grows to approximately 14 million by 1930 as radio is transformed from a long-distance signaling device to a mass medium; the golden age of radio begins

1930 Lowell Thomas, over complaints of newspapers, begins reading newspaper stories on NBC—the first regular radio network news

1933 Edwin Armstrong patents an FM radio system

1934 The Communications Act of 1934 replaces the Radio Act; the Federal Communications Commission is formed; the Mutual Radio Network begins operation

1938 Orson Welles celebrates Halloween with a broadcast describing a Martian invasion

1941 Inception of commercial FM service

1943 RCA sells its Blue Network to Edward Noble; it becomes ABC in 1945

1950s End of traditional network radio, beginning of formula (top 40) station formats

1954 First portable transistor radio sold

1958 Payola scandals hit format radio stations

1961 The FCC authorizes FM stereo

1967 The Public Broadcasting Act creates the Corporation for Public Broadcasting; National Public Radio is established in 1970

1971 Congress bans broadcasts of cigarette advertising

1979 FM's national audience exceeds AM's for the first time (by 1990s, FM serves more than 75 percent of the U.S. audience)

1981 Congress extends terms of radio licenses from three years to seven

1982 The FCC authorizes AM stereo

1987 The FCC eliminates the Fairness Doctrine

1992 The FCC eases ownership rules (duopoly and LMAs); begins legal process to authorize digital audio broadcasting (DAB)

1

Resilient Radio

Marilyn J. Matelski

"Tradition," wrote Marshall McLuhan in 1964, "is the sense of the total past as now. Its awakening is a natural result of radio impact and of electric information in general." For radio in the 1990s, with its tradition of survival and renewal, the total past *is* now, whatever the doomsayers contend. Having revolutionized a world of mass communications then dominated by print and subsequently having lost its place to an upstart offspring, television, radio is accustomed to being dismissed as dead in a modern media world dominated by images, where the visual seems to mute the aural.

Over and over again, however, reports of radio's death have proven premature. Even though "broadcasting" often seems to mean "TV" in the 1990s and radio seemingly is forgotten in the volatile electronic media mix, adaptable radio has outlived many of its skeptics.

Once the marvel of the age, the glue that held a nation together through disasters, war and economic depression, radio is now perceived by some as occupying a corner chair at the media family's gatherings, a maiden aunt, beloved but past her prime. Not so. Venerable in the family of electronic media, radio, the first broadcast medium, may also be the last as television increasingly depends on cable instead of on over-the-air signals. Far from shriveling from the media scene, there is no medium more ubiquitous than radio, no source of information, entertainment, music, sports, weather and business news more pervasive in people's lives. "To most of us, radio is as much a part of our day as morning coffee and the ride to work or school," observed broadcasting scholar Michael C. Keith. "It is a companion that keeps us informed about world and local events, gives us sports scores, provides us with the latest weather and school closings and a host of other information—not to mention our favorite music—and asks for nothing in return."

Perhaps the victim of its own success, radio is so omnipresent that it is easy to take for granted. There are 11,338 radio stations in this country and 560 million radio sets in use—5.6 radios for every U.S. household. Some 95 percent of all automobiles have radios, the Radio Advertising Bureau reports, and 96 percent of U.S. adults listen for at least three hours every day; in the process, they enter a vast network linking not only all of America but the rest of the global village as well. People throughout the world wake up with radio, go to work or school with radio, talk with radio, jog with radio, date with radio, work with radio and drive with radio. Crossing the Sinai, Bedouins listen to radio on their camels.

Despite the domination of television in the last half-century, radio still ranks high as an immediate, informative and credible medium. Radio may not always get the attention it deserves, but no one would deny its worth. In fact, few could imagine a world without radio, even though the medium is greatly transformed in the 1990s from the original, pragmatic vision of its creators at the turn of the century—a means of improving ship-to-ship and ship-to-shore communications and of expediting military operations.

The early days of radio transmission were built around a common carrier concept—receivers were used much like telephones. When the *Titanic* struck the iceberg in 1912 in that most famous of sea disasters, killing 1,500 people, the broader public suddenly became much more aware of radiotelegraphy's potential. The *Titanic*'s desperate SOS drew a rescue liner from more than 50 miles away and, in the days following the sinking, the wireless (via shoreside operators such as David Sarnoff) was the world's only link for families desperate for news of the 700 survivors aboard the *Carpathia*. After World War I, radio crystal sets and kits that converted Quaker Oats boxes into home radios became popular among hobbyists, even though there was little regular broadcasting. In 1916, Sarnoff's brainstorm, explained in his "radio music box" memo to his boss at the American Marconi Co., showed a way to convert radio from a common carrier device for maritime, commercial and government communication into a "household utility." The company could sell more wireless receivers, Sarnoff suggested, if the "radio music box" were designed to bring entertainment, sports, news, lectures and weather reports into American homes. American Marconi rejected the idea as impractical, but by 1919, Sarnoff and his new Radio Corporation of America had proved his point.

During these embryonic years of broadcasting, the radio industry structure was vague: Regulatory parameters were still undefined, "experimental" AM stations were scattered throughout the country in a crazy-quilt fashion and the concept of a radio "network" was in its infancy. Radio programs aired without commercials; the notion of seeking sponsorship to underwrite programming expenses had not yet been fully developed. Still, the early leaders in station programming—WEAF in New York, KDKA in Pittsburgh, Cincinnati's WLW and WNAC in Boston—established a baseline standard for future broadcasting with such concepts as live sports (with play-by-play announcing), radio vaudeville and music from "make-believe ballrooms."

Within a few short years, the landscape of broadcasting had changed dramatically. From Quaker Oats boxes just a few years before, Americans spent more than $350 million in 1924 on radio receivers, tubes and other hardware. By 1927, more than 500 AM radio stations had popped up across the country, eager to compete for listeners (even if it meant skipping frequencies, boosting transmission power beyond acceptable limits and airing shows with ethically questionable personalities such as the famous "goat-gland surgeon," Dr. John Brinkley). In addition, the notion of national program linkage, or "networking," had matured quickly. The National Broadcasting Company, with its Red and Blue networks, was formed in 1926 and the Columbia Broadcasting System followed in 1928.

Most significantly, advertising had become the new mantra for aspiring radio programmers. Sponsors not only purchased spot time on network and local productions in the late 1920s, but they also created their own shows and bought time to air them. In fact, advertising influence grew so quickly that, at times, a single agency could control as much as 10 percent of a network's schedule. While giving a station economic stability, this threatened programming independence. As the broadcasting industry continued to flourish, a Federal Radio Commission, later reconstituted as the Federal Communications Commission, was formed to address these rapidly growing problems by regulating technical, economic and programming matters. Radio broadcasting was subsequently identified in the 1927 Federal Radio Act as a private enterprise utilizing public airwaves. By this definition, programmers were challenged with somewhat dualistic goals: They could enjoy the benefits of a free market system as long as they served their audiences responsibly.

By the early 1930s, just two decades after its inception, broadcast radio had evolved into a major facet of American life. This phenomenon was due not only to rapid station growth, but also to the Great Depression, which put about 15 million people—one-fifth of the U.S. work force—out of work. People had little money to spend, but plenty of time to listen and a desperate need for entertainment to take their minds off their troubles. Increased demand during the Depression years powered phenomenal growth in stations and in advertising revenues, which climbed from about $40 million in 1930 at the start of the Depression to more than $112 million in 1935. This growth was particularly dramatic, considering that for most of the 1930s, total annual media advertising revenues (including newspapers, magazines, films and direct mail) dropped by half from levels prior to 1929, to less than $2 billion a year.

During these years, radio stations provided vertical programming—diversified shows with general audience appeal—and were network-dominated in all respects. The reasons for such influence were simple; the networks provided a higher production quality and more star-studded casts than most local stations could ever hope to create on their own. They also provided the interconnection between stations and much of the advertising revenue for affiliates. Local programmers usually filled in the gaps of the network schedule by dispensing regional news, sports and information, as well as by serving the community with public affairs shows, call-ins and programs of local interest.

Programming in the 1930s and '40s was creative, vibrant, diverse. The typical broadcast day consisted of first-rate comedy routines, soap operas, action thrillers and variety shows, all of which served as superb entertainment as well as providing instant fame for aspiring actors, writers, producers and directors (many of whom later used their radio experience as an entré into television). "The Fleischmann Hour," for example, a variety show hosted by Rudy Vallee, was one of several series that launched the TV careers of comic entertainers including Milton Berle, Edgar Bergen and Eddie Cantor. Even the announcers for programs such as "The Maxwell House Hour" and "The Palmolive Hour" achieved a celebrity status previously unrecognized. Ben Bernie, who emceed shows for groups such as the Cities Service Orchestra, the Cliquot Club Eskimos and the Ipana Troubadours, said "people were thunderstruck" when they met him in person. "When you said you were a radio announcer, they stared at you as if they couldn't believe that the voice coming out of the receiver actually had a body attached to it."

Comedy was perhaps the most important radio genre during the Great Depression and World War II because, as former announcer Jimmy Wallington remarked, "it brought a lot of laughter to a lot of people who needed it." "Amos 'n' Andy," for example, became so popular during these years that when the United States adopted daylight savings time, many factories changed their hours so employees could get home in time for the show. The success of "Amos 'n' Andy" was significant in other ways as well, most notably (for programmers), in its format. Previously, radio executives had believed it programmatically unwise to run storylines that were not resolved within an episode. "Amos 'n' Andy," along with other open-ended comedies like "The Goldbergs" and "Myrt and Marge," paved the way for the serial as a successful form of radio entertainment both in prime time and daytime.

Daytime dramas were as successful as their prime-time counterparts, despite concerns that an economically unattractive listening audience (housewives) would deter sponsors from purchasing advertising spot time in this scheduling block. Despite these reservations, the networks decided to experiment with several 15-minute episodes, provided to sponsors at discounts. Most advertising support for the daytime dramas came from sponsors that made household products—Colgate Palmolive-Peet and Procter and Gamble, among others. Thus, the term "soap opera" was born to describe the melodramas sold by detergent companies.

Programmers and sponsors quickly discovered that housewives, while not directly in the labor force, often controlled the household purse strings. By 1939, advertising revenue for the popular serials exceeded $26 million; today, soaps claim more than $900 million in total network revenues each year—one-sixth of all annual network profits. Housewives found daytime dramas an attractive substitute for previous program fare (such as hygienic information, recipe readings and household tips), and demonstrated their consumer power as well.

Besides entertainment, radio served to link Americans to their political leaders and news events in a way that had never been possible. When President Franklin D. Roosevelt spoke directly to the American people in regular fireside chats, he invested the medium with some of the authority of the presidency. When the German zeppelin *Hindenburg*, the world's largest airship, landed at Lakehurst, N.J., in 1937, radio was there. Herb Morrison of WLS, covering the landing, transmitted his own horror into homes across the country as the giant airship suddenly ignited: "It's burst into flames," he sobbed into the microphone. "Oh my! It's burning, bursting into flames.... Oh, the humanity, all the passengers!" And listeners shared his horror firsthand. Radio now brought not just music, comedy and the reassuring voices of presidents into Americans' living rooms, but disaster and tragedy as well.

Given radio's place as a trusted and valued member of the family, as well as its status as a voice of authority, it perhaps was understandable that so many Americans on October 30, 1938, believed they were about to be killed by Martians when the radio told them so. Some 6 million people were listening to CBS's "Mercury Theater on the Air" when ballroom music was interrupted by authoritative-sounding accounts of an invasion of horrible creatures from Mars, whose spaceships started landing in Grover's Mill, N.J. Listeners panicked as radio reported that Martian death rays had killed millions, and heard one radio announcer vaporized on the air. The show's creator, Orson Welles, later said he'd had no idea that listeners would believe the Halloween radio play was real. But for many, the "War of the Worlds" underscored the dangerous potential of radio.

By the beginning of World War II, many Americans had become accustomed to receiving their information via radio, along with their newspapers and movie theater newsreels. Part of the reason was its style; audiences loved to listen to the dramatic voices of H.V. Kaltenborn, Boake Carter and Gabriel Heatter, and also wanted to hear the commentators' opinions about the issues of the day. These familiar personalities made listeners feel knowledgeable and in control of world affairs. The charismatic Walter Winchell was perhaps the most noteworthy example of such presence; media critic Barbara Matusow estimates that Winchell often attracted more than 25 million loyal fans a night with his unique blend of news, gossip and innuendo.

In the late 1930s, CBS President William S. Paley commissioned Edward R. Murrow to recruit a cadre of radio journalists for war coverage in Europe. Murrow assembled some of the best talent in the world—William L. Shirer, Howard K. Smith, Robert Trout, Larry LeSuer, Eric

Sevareid, George Polk, Richard C. Hottelet, David Schoenbrun, Walter Cronkite and Charles Collingwood. This brilliant team perfected radio news broadcasting in Europe and then elevated it to an art form in the United States. While NBC was also heavily involved in wartime reporting (many competitors often rode in the same jeeps as Murrow's CBS teams), no one could compete with Murrow's stature. He and his CBS colleagues, broadcasting live from the German Reichstag or from London rooftops during the Blitz, made World War II real for most Americans. A 1945 poll taken by the National Opinion Research Center at the University of Chicago found that 61 percent of Americans said they received most of their news from radio, compared to 35 percent who favored newspapers. These findings most certainly were due in part to Murrow, who epitomized the ideal of radio reporting with integrity as well as feeling.

Despite its prestigious status for over four decades, radio's popularity began to slip after the war. Advertisers had fewer dollars to spend, leaving network programming departments with less extravagant budgets. But most important in radio's slump was the advent of radio's electronic offspring, television, in the late 1940s.

Television was introduced officially to the American public in 1939, when, on camera, FDR opened the New York World's Fair. Spectators were delighted by the new device. Despite distribution difficulties during World War II, media critics prophesied that TV would quickly overtake its electronic predecessor, radio; some even predicted that radio would become a forgotten medium within a decade. Soon it seemed the gloomy forecast might be correct. By 1950, more than 4 million television sets had replaced the console radio's honored place in American living rooms. As historian Joshua E. Mills recorded in his book, *Radio in the Television Age*, newsmagazines such as *Business Week* began to chronicle radio's demise with headlines like "Radio Rates Start to Crack" (April 28, 1951), "TV Is Hot on Radio's Heels" (May 24, 1952) and "Network Revenue: Down, Down, Down" (July 17, 1954).

"Radio stations had a terrible time keeping personnel," former NBC Radio President Jack Thayer later told Mills. "Everybody wanted to get into television. They would leave and go do anything—salespeople, sales managers, program people.... It was like vaudeville when films began. Management left, technicians left. It was like rats deserting a sinking ship."

But unlike its signals, radio didn't fade into the ether. Instead, station owners redefined the medium to fit the new pragmatics—lower budgets, less live talent, smaller audiences. The first step was to look at radio's strengths: It required less equipment to operate and was much more portable than television, especially after the development of transistors in 1948. In addition, while local AM stations had proliferated for several decades, TV had just begun to be recognized as a local influence (and even then, only in large markets). Further, radio had led a nation through depression and war; its reputation as a valued citizen was beyond reproach.

Clearly, the most serious threat was economic. Television, newer and more seductive, lured audiences, advertisers and industry talent from its less flashy older sibling. Even so, the financial landscape was not entirely bleak; despite lower station revenues, manufacturers and owners still had a vested interest in radio's solvency. As for advertising support, industry income remained solid—even in 1954, one of the worst financial years in radio history, advertising revenues topped more than $450 million.

Local radio operators set about to create a new image and find new niches. Without network programming, most local stations could not afford to underwrite large variety shows or dramas, so they turned instead to prerecorded music with live personalities, called "record jockeys," (or, as *Variety* later dubbed them, "disc jockeys") as hosts. The industry also decided to settle its long-standing feud with the recording business to the mutual benefit of each. Finally, radio visionaries recognized that the notion of programming to mass audiences—or "broadcasting"—was no longer a reality for the medium; instead, stations began to identify target audiences and create formats to "narrowcast" to those listeners. By the mid-'50s, specialized programming had proliferated, with different formats—rock 'n' roll (top 40), jazz, classical, country-western, pop, gospel and bluegrass/folk—developed to appeal to many listener tastes. While some full service (vertically programmed) stations still existed, providing varied informational and entertainment content, the true future of radio was clearly to be found in specialization (horizontal programming) as well as in localism.

Strong local identity was essential to radio's stability and growth in the television age, and station programmers seized every opportunity to demonstrate commitment to their communities. A 1954 report by the

National Association of Radio and Television Broadcasters noted that in addition to such activities as publicity campaigns for new libraries and better highways, reports of local news and activities had "assumed major proportions, [making] up about 40 percent of all news broadcasts on the average station." Retooling the medium by combining strong local identity and specialized programming was enough to save radio from its TV-induced slide. Critics who had earlier sounded the death knell for radio began to take notice, not only of radio's adaptability to a changing technological world, but also of its innovative programming aimed at specific segments of American society—notably teen-agers—that had previously been ignored.

In addition to creating formats to compete with TV, radio has had to weather crises within its own industry as well, mostly technological. The most significant of these was the rise of FM radio in the 1970s. Since FM stations operate at a higher frequency than AM, and consequently are less vulnerable to interference, the FM signal was much clearer and hence more popular with music listeners. Within a decade after its inception in 1969, FM's annual revenues skyrocketed from $67.4 million to over $700 million in 1981. In the 1990s, FM radio claims as much as 85 percent of the listening audience and challenges AM's very survival. AM is hanging on, however, and some radio industry experts believe that the real programming innovations in the next few years will occur at AM stations, although both AM and FM continue to target their programming for specific audiences.

Radio has also survived the economic downturn of the late 1980s and early '90s. After taking its lumps during the 1980s era of inflated leveraged buyouts and their subsequent crashes, radio still appears to be the best mass media buy for advertisers because of its comparatively low costs and targeted programming. In fact, industry forecasters such as Veronis, Suhler and Associates predict radio advertising revenues of over $12 billion by 1995.

Specialization became the name of the radio survival game in the 1990s. In 1992, *Broadcasting/Cable Yearbook* listed more than 60 formats throughout the country, including "eskimo," "new wave" and "Elvis," in addition to a wide array of music formats, talk/news, sports, Christian and many others. Meanwhile, some 37 syndication companies offer more than 200 programs for specialized interests, including joke services for DJs, "Funeral Focus" and "Louis L'Amour Theater." Some broadcast critics, however, suggest that too much specialization may not be a good thing. Horizontal programming, while ensuring radio's economic survival, permits stations to focus so narrowly on specific audience demographics that many no longer consider the broader general public interest, some observers say.

Other controversial regulatory issues such as local marketing agreements, duopolistic ownership, as well as new technologies (especially satellite transmission and digital audio broadcasting) still challenge radio's ability to adjust to and survive in an increasingly complex media world. But the "radio music box" has already proven itself adaptable when faced with technological or economic change.

Doomsayers may question radio's future direction but cannot doubt its future. Radio, venerable in the family of electronic media, may be so common as to have become part of the woodwork. But its very ubiquity, resilience and diversity are proof that the box that brought us the London Blitz, baseball, "The Lone Ranger," "All Things Considered," the Beatles, rap, hip-hop, Rush Limbaugh, "a day that will live in infamy" and hundreds more is no more likely to become a forgotten medium in the 1990s than it was in the 1950s.

Marilyn J. Matelski, professor of communication at Boston College, is author of several books on broadcast programming, including The Soap Opera Evolution *and* TV News Ethics.

2

Looking Back at Radio's Future

B. Eric Rhoads

Ever since the passing of radio's golden era, when it was the only mass entertainment medium, radio has been considered by cynics to be in decline. In the 1950s, golden-age hangers-on tried to keep the medium alive with radio drama—shows like "Dragnet." But successful radio no longer included live radio drama and variety shows—the era of format music radio had come to meet what consumers wanted, and efforts to update the formulas that had made radio golden in the 1930s were no match for television.

Once television took hold and the American public "abandoned" radio, fascination with pictures dominated. Over the past 50 years, nothing has been able to overcome the perception that television's birth meant radio's death. But radio's death—if that's what it is—has been a lingering one. In the first of many reprieves, the advent of rock 'n' roll in the 1950s revived listener interest, bringing back the youth market and giving radio a new hook, a new reason to listen. Developed by music radio legends Gordon McLendon and Todd Storz, the endless top-40 hits and promotions were like pied pipers, enticing new generations to the radio dial. The 1960s gave birth to great stations like KHJ Los Angeles, WRKO Boston and CKLW Detroit, which became the standard for thousands of bad 30-song sets without interruptions, on-air personalities sounded like clones. Radio had caught up with itself again.

In the 1990s, having abandoned personality programming when the golden age was done and moved like lemmings in one homogenized format direction or another, radio now seems to have come full circle, back to personalities. Larry King, Rush Limbaugh, Charles Adler,

Howard Stern, The Greaseman, G. Gordon Liddy and others are money in the bank. And they're relatively unassailable: you can't duplicate a personality, only go head-to-head with another personality who might draw better.

Given that, the copycat trend now manifests itself in new ways. Rather than hiring a DJ with orders to be as controversial as Howard Stern, for instance, stations can get the genuine article, Stern himself, via satellite. Rather than remaking a hot format, copied from a successful station in another market, operators can drop in satellite-delivered programming in its original form with its original on-air people. In some cases, they can rebroadcast the entire air sound of a successful station. You want to sound like WSIX/Nashville? Buy it through syndication and insert your own call letters.

But even this new innovation in the quest for a distinctive and successful sound is just another turn around the old hampster wheel. Eventually, Stern or Limbaugh or the latest fave rave will be everywhere, thanks to syndication and satellites, and competitors will be looking for new wrinkles that will make their stations stand out from the pack. Over the next five years, more new formats and variations on those already in existence will spring up. Radio fragmentation will become more geared to lifestyle groups, social groups and economic groups, creating formats and meeting the needs of each. Mass-marketed stations will become fewer and farther between. Joining the plethora of formats carried on every radio dial—talk, country, news, classic album, easy listening, rap, urban, top 40 (now called contemporary hit radio—CHR), adult album, adult contemporary, lite rock, jazz, oldies (country oldies, rock oldies, soul oldies...), sports—will be new formats—teen talk, ethnic, children's, "alternative lifestyle," for women only, for men only, etc. Many have been tried, but the timing or need was wrong. The near future will provide an environment ripe for more programming alternatives.

Fragmentation is the way of the media world. Magazine racks are filled with thousands of choices, and radio has followed in that direction with something for everyone. One new wrinkle is cable radio, which already offers 30 channels, with 30 more expected this year—60 formats, uninterrupted by commercials and DJs, with digital sound quality. Since there aren't 60 formats in radio, narrow versions are being offered—all-vocal classical, Latin ballads, show tunes, traditional gospel music, contemporary gospel music, etc. With its vast channel capacity and flawless sound quality, cable radio could threaten local radio, except for one weakness: it's not portable. Broadcast radio can go wherever the listener goes: to the beach, the garage, the car, the jogging trail, to isolated campsites, anywhere. Because of this, broadcast radio will survive (again), although in-home listening might decline in upscale households. The obvious solution for radio is to get away from jukebox-style programming, nonpersonality homogenization and to focus on localism.

The advent of many new electronic technologies offers challenges and opportunities for a radio culture that has shown itself so quick to evolve and adapt to new market and technological conditions. Here, the future of radio is a brave new world of threats and promise. The major threat is the rapidly changing nature of technology, changes so rapid that obsolescence sets in by the time some products reach the market. The new developments are many:

• *Digital compression* technology means that electronic products that were once hopelessly sophisticated for the market now need little more than a good computer programmer to be practical. Automation is now so sophisticated that taped local personalities can be heard on local automated stations indistiguishable from live programming. With satellite technology, stations can operate without people, with all technical requirements handled by computer or satellite-monitoring services. A complete radio station can be housed in a closet.

• *Regional radio* companies with multiple stations and markets will create their own regional satellite networks as the low cost of satellite uplinks will allow virtually anyone to feed programming to affiliates, with localization in each market. Thus, six (or 60) stations could originate from one location, each adding its own local news and local community activities, with sales and business functions handled centrally. Technology will also create new format possibilities. A Fresno, Calif., station has created a sophisticated software program allowing the station to do classified radio: Listeners call in, record a classified ad and push the phone button corresponding to the category (such as automotive) in which it should be played. They press another number to indicate how many times they want the ad to run. Charges appear on their phone bill, so the station doesn't have to do any billing or collecting. For an AM station with a single employee and no other format prospects, it's an ideal solution.

• *Direct broadcast satellite* (DBS) transmission will make it possible to broadcast a signal from a satellite to a home or car radio receiver, which will create a number of "national" radio stations that can be received like a local station once the Federal Communications Commission approves the plan.

• *Digital audio broadcasting* (DAB) is another change soon expected to win FCC approval. Essentially, DAB will create a new band of CD-quality digital audio. The dilemma is over allocation of the limited DAB spectrum, a question that surely will continue to generate heat. It's unlikely that everyone will win, because the total of all FMs and AMs exceeds the available number of DAB channels. Although DAB systems are said to allow simultaneous broadcast of DAB and FM or AM signals, eventually AM and FM will be phased out, a prospect based on FCC actions and the market proliferation of receivers capable of handling DAB.

• *Another new wrinkle* radio broadcast data service (RBDS), a technology permitting data transmission over radio signals. Used in Europe for years, radios can be set to receive special interruptions—traffic reports, news bulletins, etc.—and feature a miniature LED screen that can display data. Listeners will be able to insert a credit card-size memory card into their radio, press a button, record the name of the song or an advertiser coupon and take the card to a retailer to redeem the coupon or purchase the recording.

• *Recent FCC rulings* allow companies to own more radio stations in a market (duopolies) and to lease airtime from competing stations (local marketing agreements, or LMAs). The jury is still out on the success of these measures. As one broadcaster put it, "If you can't run one station successfully, what makes you think you can run more than one successfully?" Still, many in the industry think duopoly and LMA rules will reduce the number of radio competitors in a marketplace and make survival more likely, thus making radio more profitable.

• *Advertisers* are looking at radio differently than in recent years. In the past, radio has been a difficult buy because of the number of choices and formats, but today, radio is the most stable of media. It can be targeted by lifestyle formats and is more efficient than other mediums from a cost and production standpoint. As a result, many major advertising agencies are moving more of their budgets into radio. Radio's strong local bond with its listeners bodes well for advertisers that have seen other media become more distanced from their audience. Suddenly, a choice of 40 radio stations in a market seems a lot easier and more concentrated than a choice of 60 to 100 (or more) cable channels.

With the country's changing social and cultural makeup, radio's role—as always—is adapting to reflect the changing tastes and needs of consumers. As a reflective, reactive medium, radio's proven ability to adapt to the needs of the society and the marketplace, and to react quickly to events, places it at the forefront of media as we approach a new century. In the 1990s, radio confronts the same challenges—social, economic, technological—as the rest of the country. But its immediacy, local identity and portability give it an edge on competing media.

An economic downturn and policies permitting over-licensure of radio stations mean that radio's health and future are threatened at the end of the century that saw its birth. But duopoly and LMA legislation promised to redress issues of radio's overpopulation (although the Clinton administration is said to be considering reversing those FCC actions). If duopoly and LMA regulations are left in place, radio broadcasters have a chance to make a living in otherwise losing economic situations.

Technically speaking, radio must wait for decisions and implementation of new technologies. Success will depend on the coordination of these efforts with receiver manufacturers so that consumers do not find themselves with obsolete equipment as the capabilities expand. Radio also faces technical choices that will allow more efficient operations and more programming choices than ever before possible.

Ultimately, the future for radio is promising. As always, it is resilient and market-sensitive. Still cost efficient and effective as an advertising medium, radio is as profitable a media prospect—socially and economically speaking—as at any time in the last 10 years. Though not a forgotten medium, radio is taken for granted. Like the power company, you don't realize how important it is until you flip the switch and it's not there.

B. Eric Rhoads is publisher of Radio Ink, *an industry magazine produced in Boynton Beach, Fla.*

3

Radio's Political Past

Michael X. Delli Carpini

The history of radio is inextricably suffused with politics. Though licensed experimental stations were transmitting as early as 1916, the first scheduled and advertised radio program in America—broadcast on November 2, 1920, from Pittsburgh's KDKA—was an 18-hour marathon on the election returns of the Harding-Cox presidential race. Over the following months, KDKA broadcast numerous other civic-oriented programs.

In November 1921, radio beamed the voice of the U.S. president overseas for the first time when RCA's powerful Port Jefferson, Long Island, station went on the air with an international address by President Harding that was heard by radio listeners in Europe, Japan, Australia and Central and South America. While Harding was the first president to use radio as a means of political communication, Calvin Coolidge—who succeeded Harding on his death in August 1923—was more adept at it, a fact Coolidge recognized. "I am very fortunate that I came in with the radio," Coolidge commented. "I can't make an engaging, rousing or oratorical speech...but I have a good radio voice, and now I can get my message across to [the public] without acquainting them with my lack of oratorical ability."

Radio was initially viewed as a public, democratic medium. In May 1922, the premiere issue of *Radio Broadcast* heralded radio as "the people's university," a public resource that would make government "a living thing to its citizens." Media historian Erik Barnouw said the new medium symbolized the "coming of age of the enlightenment.... It would link rich and poor, young and old. It would end the isolation of rural life. It would unite the nation."

For a few years following KDKA's initial broadcast, American radio came remarkably close to this utopian vision. The 400 stations that quickly arose around the country were run largely by public, civic and religious institutions. Broadcasts ran the gamut from culture to politics, but the idea of mass and continuing education was paramount: in 1922 alone, 70 college and university stations went on the air. And since the profits from radio were assumed to derive from the sale of radio receivers, none of these first 400 stations sold airtime for any purpose. Indeed the idea of selling the air—of "ether advertising"—was, for a brief period at least, inconceivable.

This golden age was short-lived. In August 1922, AT&T went on the air in New York City with WEAF (later to become WNBC), the first of several "toll broadcast" stations. Based on the logic of telephones, WEAF was viewed as a kind of phone booth (a "radiotelephone") in which anyone could—for a fee—broadcast a message to a listening audience. These messages could be commercial or noncommercial, entertainment or educational. Initial reaction to this approach was almost universally negative. The government of New York City, when told that it would have to pay to broadcast civic messages, refused, opting instead to purchase its own transmitter. Secretary of Commerce Herbert Hoover, given responsibility to regulate radio by way of a vague 1912 statute, said, "It is inconceivable that we should allow so great a possibility for service... to be drowned in advertising chatter," and later warned that the civic value of broadcasting would be lost if presidential messages became "the meat in a sandwich of two patent medicine advertisements." Nonetheless, the commercial value of the airwaves became obvious when a real estate developer reported increased sales of $127,000 after paying $50 for a 10-minute promotional spot on WEAF.

The shift from a medium dominated by public interests to one dominated by private ones was inexorable as commercialization made it difficult for nonprofit stations to compete for talent or audiences. Commercial stations, bolstered by profits and corporate backing, literally drowned out public stations with their more powerful transmitters. AT&T's extensive cable hookups allowed it to "network" stations around the country, thus creating regional and then national audiences. Government regulation during this time also worked to the disadvantage of the noncommercial stations, which were viewed as "less public" than "toll" stations that were theoretically available to anyone willing (and able) to pay for airtime. Thus, commercial stations such as WEAF were granted "clear channel" frequencies (assuring signals that were free from interference and that allowed the use of powerful transmitters), while educational stations were given "local" frequencies with severe restrictions in power and, in some cases, in the hours when they could broadcast. Noncommercial stations were unable to compete in this environment. By 1927, only 90 of the 732 radio stations in operation were run by educational institutions and two years later, 44 of those had gone off the air. Despite several efforts during the Roosevelt administration to reorient the radio industry toward the public good, by the 1930s the idea of radio as "the people's university" was dead.

Throughout this period, radio's more explicitly political value continued to evolve, often with mixed results. The broadcasting of the 1924 Democratic Convention proved a public relations nightmare, taking an unprecedented 103 ballots to nominate John W. Davis as the party's compromise presidential candidate. The listening audience also suffered through a bitter battle over the relationship of the Ku Klux Klan to the Democratic Party and the unsuccessful attempt of vice presidential nominee William Jennings Bryan to translate his significant oratorical skills to radio. Radio proved a poor medium for Davis as well—as one observer noted, "Mr. Davis...has a voice which to the direct auditor has that bell-like quality of his delightful rhetoric. Via radio, however, this muffles and fogs...." By campaign's end, Davis commented that radio "will make the long speech impossible or inadvisable...the short speech will be in vogue."

Both the promise and the limits of early radio could be found in the 1924 presidential campaign of Progressive Party candidate Robert LaFollette, who wrote that radio "will undoubtedly serve to minimize misrepresentation in the news columns of the press." His campaign made frequent use of the airwaves and his Labor Day address is credited as the first political speech delivered exclusively for a radio audience. Nonetheless, LaFollette also charged that the "radio trust" conspired during the campaign to keep him and his progressive, anti-monopoly message off the airwaves.

Not surprisingly, the most effective use of radio in the 1924 presidential campaign was made by Republican Calvin Coolidge. "Silent Cal's" broadcasts "went straight to the popular heart," one observer commented. "During the campaign he had little to say and said it well." This approach was no coincidence. The Republicans understood better than either the Democrats or the Progressives that radio changed the way in which a campaign should be structured. They largely abandoned the traditional "barnstorming" technique in favor of radio addresses broadcast simultaneously by several stations (Coolidge's final campaign speech was broadcast by a then-record 26 stations). They also saw that radio provided greater flexibility to campaign strategy and allowed for a "big push" late in the campaign. An internal memo prepared as an outline of the party's strategy for using radio presciently noted that "broadcasting requires a new type of sentence. Its language is not that of the platform orator.... Speeches must be short. Ten minutes is a limit and five minutes is better."

The Republicans outspent Democrats 3-to-1 on radio broadcasts in the 1924 election. The Grand Old Party even opened its own radio station in New York, broadcasting all day and evening from late October until election day. In addition, radio stations (especially those with the most powerful transmitters) were disproportionately owned by conservative business interests and so were especially sympathetic to the Republicans' message. As a result, Republicans were heard on the airwaves three to four times more often than Democrats and eight to 10 times more often than Progressives. In the end, Coolidge won the presidency with 382 electoral votes and nearly 16 million popular votes—twice Davis' total. The age of the electronic campaign had arrived.

Coolidge made even greater use of radio during his second administration than he had during his limited first term. His 1925 inaugural address was heard by a record 15 million Americans and during that year he averaged 9,000 words a month over the airwaves. Thanks to this new medium, "Silent Cal" was heard by more citizens than all the prior presidents combined. Indeed, the president came in fourth in a poll of most-liked "radio personalities," ahead of consummate radio entertainer Will Rogers. Despite his frequent use of the radio, however, Coolidge limited his addresses to prepared speeches and formal events such as the State of the Union address, eschewing more extemporaneous exchanges or informal conversations. "I don't think it's necessary for the president periodically to address the country by radio," he announced at one press conference.

The 1928 presidential race pitted Republican Herbert Hoover against Democrat Alfred Smith, neither particularly effective radio speakers. Radio stations began charging candidates for airtime, but both campaigns still employed radio fairly extensively, including several innovative uses of the medium. The Republicans, for example, created a half-hour radio address that summarized the party's major positions. This prepared speech was then delivered by well-known local citizens (from public officials to a neighborhood butcher) on 174 community radio stations around the nation. The Democrats opted for a mix of low-brow and high-brow culture, with one broadcast featuring vaudeville stars extolling Smith's virtues to the tune of "East Side, West Side," and second a more serious broadcast of a radio play based on Smith's life. The 1928 campaign also featured a series of nonpartisan programs sponsored by the League of Women Voters. Called the "Voter's Campaign Information Service," these weekly broadcasts reached about 20 million voters over a 22-station hookup and were intended to give citizens information ranging from how the nominating process worked to the candidates' stands on issues. Although Democrats outspent Republicans for radio advertising, Hoover won a landslide victory in 1928, and for all the attention paid to radio advertising, total spending amounted to only 18 percent of the Democratic National Committee's total campaign budget and only 10 percent of the Republicans', even though radio was able to reach 40 million listeners by 1928, as compared to only a few million in 1924.

By the late 1920s and early 1930s, radio had become a standard part of public officials' communications arsenal. More than 100 congressional speeches aired during the 1929–1930 term, with Hoover adding 37 of his own, and that number increased as the nation plunged deeper into economic depression. By the end of his term, Hoover had made 95 radio addresses, only nine fewer than FDR would make during his first term of office. While not a particularly effective radio speaker, Hoover's long-term involvement in the development and regulation of radio gave him a keen understanding of the medium's power.

"Radio has become a social force of the first order," Hoover reflected. "It is revolutionizing the political debates that underlie political action under our principles of government.... [It] physically makes us literally one people upon all occasions of general public interest." Toward the end of his presidency, however, aware that even the power of radio could not restore public confidence in his administration, Hoover commented that "it is very difficult to deal with anything over the radio except generalities."

Hoover's 1932 reelection bid began with a radio address broadcast over a record 160-station hookup. Overall, the Republican presidential campaign used a total of 73 hours of network broadcasting time, up from 1928's 43 hours. In contrast, the cash-poor Democrats could buy only 52 hours of airtime, slightly *less* than they had purchased four years earlier. Even so, Hoover was no match for Franklin Delano Roosevelt as a radio orator, the latter having been selected by broadcasting officials as the best political speaker in the nation. Broadcasters lauded FDR's "ability to create a feeling of intimacy between himself and his listeners, [and] his adroitness in presenting complicated matters in such simple terms that the man in the street believes he has full mastery of them." But Hoover sounded like "an old-fashioned phonograph in need of winding."

In many ways, the 1930s and '40s marked the zenith of radio's political impact. Central to this impact were FDR's "fireside chats," a series of 28 radio addresses spread over his three full terms in office. These addresses, pointed attempts to rally public support for pending legislation as well as more discursive reviews and explanations of government actions, ranged in length from 15 to 45 minutes, usually broadcast on weeknights between 9 and 11 p.m. The audience varied, though a 1940 opinion poll indicated that 60 percent of the adult population had listened to a Roosevelt radio broadcast at least once during his first two terms in office. One address, in which he proclaimed a bank holiday (as a way of slowing the run on money), was heard on 64 percent of the radios around the country—a record that still holds today.

The political use of radio during the 1930s extended well beyond the fireside chats, however. For example, FDR's eight chats delivered from 1933 to 1936 represent less than 8 percent of his radio addresses during his first term; over the first 10 months of that term alone, Roosevelt made 20 radio addresses, Eleanor Roosevelt made 17, and members of his cabinet made more than 100 addresses. Nor was this extensive use of radio limited to members of the executive branch—in 1934, NBC and CBS provided free airtime to U.S. senators 150 times, to congressmen 200 times, and to governors more than 50 times. Not surprisingly, the vast majority of these broadcasts spoke in favor of the New Deal, bringing charges from Republicans of partisan manipulation of the airwaves.

Throughout the 1930s, political debate was enlivened by the radio commentary of progressives like Hans Von Kaltenborn, Dorothy Thompson and Edward R. Murrow, and of conservatives such as Boake Carter, Upton Close and Fulton Lewis Jr. While FDR remained king of the political airwaves, several other "radio personalities" emerged during the 1930s to challenge his reign. Most prominent among these were U.S. Sen. (and former Louisiana governor) Huey Long and Father Charles Coughlin, the "radio priest." Long, a firebrand populist whose "share our wealth" philosophy advocated a radically redistributive tax policy, combined earthy language, biblical references and working class vernacular to appeal to the masses. A master at the use of political slogans (for example, "every man a king!"), he seemed destined to have a major impact on national politics until his assassination in 1935. Nonetheless, the "Kingfish's" effective use of both local and national radio and the resulting growth in his popularity are viewed by many as having pushed Roosevelt farther to the political left than might have been his natural proclivity.

Less easily categorized but no less skilled a radio orator was Father Charles Coughlin. From an obscure beginning broadcasting over a local Detroit radio station in 1926, Coughlin built a national following for his eclectic, often inconsistent, mix of populism, socialism and religion. At base, however, was an appeal similar to that of Long and, in a different way, to FDR: the promise of a better life for the many "common folk" who had been devastated by the Depression. Coughlin's radio style was dramatic. "He manages always to speak as though his words of warning were being uttered just two jumps ahead of the crack of doom," a contemporary observed. Initially a supporter of Roosevelt and the New Deal, he broke with FDR in 1935, charging him with being "in love with the international bankers" and "wedded basically to the philosophy of the money changers." In 1936, the radio priest backed the third-party candidacy of William Lemke, and also applied pressure on Congress; for example, the Senate was deluged with 200,000 telegrams after Coughlin attacked the World Court in one of his radio addresses. By the late 1930s Coughlin's influence had waned, however, due in part to negative reactions to anti-Semitic remarks he made during his broadcasts. Partly as a result of these remarks, the National Association of Broadcasting ruled that he had violated a ban on purchasing airtime for discussing "controversial public issues." In 1940, unable to persuade enough stations to

sell him time for commenting on the upcoming national elections, the
radio priest was forced from the airwaves.

Local radio was also swept up in the populist sentiments of the 1930s.
During the 1932 elections, Madison, Wis., station WHA gave free airtime to the Democrats, Republicans, Progressive Republicans, Socialists and Prohibitionists. More remarkably, each party was given equal
time regardless of its relative electoral strength. In 1932, WHA also
began broadcasting "Your Wisconsin Government," a regular program
aimed at educating citizens about state politics, government and policy
concerns. Even floor debates of the state legislature could be heard over
the Wisconsin airwaves.

Roosevelt's three reelection campaigns provided little drama regard-
ing their outcome but did introduce several innovations in radio poli-
ticking, many by the Republicans. In 1936, the GOP aired a "debate"
between a live Sen. Arthur Vandenberg and recorded FDR excerpts.
Twenty-one of the 66 stations that had agreed to carry the "debate" cut it
off, apparently unaware it had been staged until air time. The Republicans also made extensive use of the first campaign "spots" in 1936.
"Make it brief and people will remember what you've said" was their
operating principle (by the 1940s both parties were making extensive
use of one-minute campaign spots, often employing Hollywood talent
to produce them). And Chicago's WGN broadcast a Republican-inspired
radio drama called "Liberty at the Crossroads," in which historical and
fictional characters expressed thinly veiled criticisms of the New Deal.

By the 1940s radio had become the dominant political medium in
America. A 1940 poll by the American Institute of Public Opinion found
that 52 percent of the public used radio as their main source of political
information, compared to 38 percent who depended mainly on newspapers. Some 80 million citizens gathered around their radio sets as FDR
recounted "the day that would live in infamy" when Japan attacked.
Throughout the war Roosevelt used the radio, first to build public support for American involvement and later to both inform the public and
boost morale, and continued—though in reduced fashion—to address
domestic issues.

With Roosevelt's death in 1945, Harry Truman assumed the presidency. As a radio speaker, Truman was no FDR, as he himself noted: "I
don't think there is anybody in the country who had as rotten a delivery

as I to begin with." Careful coaching and recorded dry runs improved Truman's style, but even at his best he was only an average public speaker. The 1948 presidential campaign, the last to take place prior to the introduction of television, provided few new wrinkles, although Truman's first (and only) full term in office also introduced the first prerecorded broadcasts of presidential press conferences.

The early 1950s marked the end of radio's political reign, with television quickly emerging as the dominant form of political communication. While many of the "great moments" in political broadcasting (for example Joe McCarthy's anti-communist tirades or Richard Nixon's "Checkers" speech) were aired on both radio and television, sound alone was no match for TV's arresting images. The experience with radio also made television's introduction into the world of politics a rapid one— Edward R. Murrow's "Hear It Now" quickly became "See It Now," and the first television "polispots" were aired by Dwight Eisenhower and Adlai Stevenson during the 1952 presidential campaign. As with the rise of radio, the new medium meant a change in what defined a good communicator. The classic example of this was the first presidential debate of the 1960 campaign. By most accounts—including several formal studies—a majority of radio listeners thought Richard Nixon clearly won the debate, but television viewers, apparently reacting to Nixon's sweating brow, darting eyes and inappropriately colored suit, thought the cooler John F. Kennedy carried the day.

That television has dominated politics since the 1950s is indisputable. Television advertising is the largest single budget item in national campaigns and is increasingly dominant in state and local races as well. The television is on in the average home for more than eight hours daily, watched by adults an average of two to three hours a day. Watching television is the most preferred evening activity among Americans, even over spending time with the family. It is also the most trusted source of information for most Americans. The great moments of American politics and society over the past four decades are captured by images, not words or sounds: Kruschev at the United Nations, pounding the table with his shoe while boasting that the Soviet Union would "bury" America; peaceful civil rights protestors being attacked by police dogs and water hoses; the assassination of John F. Kennedy and the murder of Lee Harvey Oswald; the civil rights and anti-war marches in Washington; buddhist monks self-immolating and American soldiers using pocket lighters to set fire to Vietnamese huts; a human being setting foot on the moon; the Challenger space shuttle exploding before a nation's eyes; a high-tech war carried live 24 hours a day; Los Angeles' finest unmercifully beating a black citizen.

It would be a mistake, however, to discount the continued power and promise of radio. In the United States today there are more than 11,000 radio stations, the majority of them independently owned. Political and social commentary continues to reach large radio audiences, and talk radio has become an important outlet for the *vox populi*, having played a role in shaping public policy in areas ranging from congressional pay raises and catastrophic health care, and having fueled the candidacies of Ross Perot and Bill Clinton. Presidents Reagan, Bush and Clinton have made effective use of nationally syndicated weekly radio broadcasts (it was prior to one live broadcast that Ronald Reagan, unaware that his microphone was on, joked that he was about to order a nuclear attack on the Soviet Union). Public radio networks such as National Public Radio and Pacifica provide alternative slants on the news of the day, as do two black-oriented networks (Sheridan and the National Black Network) and one latino network (Caballero).

Radio's mix of networks and independents give it a unique ability to reach both large audiences and yet still cater to diverse cultural and political interests. On the one hand network broadcasts like the Larry King show can be heard by millions of listeners over more than 1,000 affiliates. On the other hand, low-power radio stations allow for extremely localized community programming. Radio may never fulfill its promise as "the people's university" and may never dominate political discourse the way it did in the 1930s and 1940s. But it remains a critical source of information and important stimulus for public discourse.

Michael X. Delli Carpini is assistant professor of political science at Barnard College in New York City.

4

News Radio—More Than Masters of Disaster

David Bartlett

Radio news is everywhere—in the car, at home, in offices, on the street, in restaurants and stores—everywhere. Fast, easy and user-friendly, radio is the dependable modern-day town crier of society's news in good times and bad. When hurricanes hit, when traffic is snarled, when the World Trade Towers are bombed, when the Orioles are in town—give radio 22 minutes (or less) and get the world.

Most Americans depend on radio news every day, which may be one reason so many take it for granted. Radio has been around for so long and has become such a familiar feature on the media landscape that we no longer pay it much conscious attention. We count on radio to be there for us whenever and wherever we want it and, paradoxically, notice it only when it isn't around.

With all the glitz of new media technologies, some say radio's days are numbered (a prediction that has been repeated for four decades). But Americans bought 71 *million* radios in 1992 (including 38.3 million battery-operated models) for a total of $2.6 *billion*. There are 22 percent more radios in this country than there were in 1980, reports Arbitron, the firm that produces the most widely used radio audience estimates, more than five for every household in the country. And Statistical Research Inc., a firm that tracks national listening patterns for the radio networks, says that 95 percent of Americans listen to radio an average of three hours and 20 minutes every day. With numbers like those, radio doesn't *sound* like a dying medium.

A key component of radio, of course, is news, the medium's ability to get essential, breaking information out to people fast, when it happens, when they need it. The master of disaster, Americans got an early under-standing of radio's utility when wireless operators in 1912 transferred names of 700 *Titanic* survivors, rescued by the *Carpathia*, to their loved ones ashore. More recently, radio was there with essential information to help Dade County hurricane victims even as the storm struck, and when the earthquake hit Los Angeles in early 1994 or shook San Fran-cisco in 1991. There's no way of knowing how many transistor radios there were in offices of the 107-story World Trade Towers when the car bomb exploded there in February 1993, cutting power and trapping thou-sands in dark and smoke, but New York radio flooded the airwaves with rescue information for those trapped inside and a 1-800 number for worried families to call. A recent survey by Bruskin-Goldring Research found that more than 40 percent of Americans over the age of 12 con-sider radio their major source of morning news, twice the number who say they depend on a morning newspaper. The same survey reported that half the population turns to radio as its principal source of informa-tion in an emergency. When the power goes out and the telephone wires are down, portable radios link us to information we need, so it's no sur-prise that 78 percent of U.S. households have battery-powered radios. When disaster strikes and usual channels of communication are cut, ra-dio remains our most reliable means of keeping in touch with the out-side world.

More than a generation ago, television was supposed to replace ra-dio. Faced with the exploding popularity of an appliance that the audi-ence could watch as well as listen to, radio station operators bailed out by the thousands.

But radio was slow to "die," and still demonstrates reluctance to go gentle into that good night the skeptics had predicted for it. The total number of commercial U.S. radio stations (even AMs) continues to climb, more than doubling from 1960 to 9,746 in 1992. In response to changing economic conditions and shifting audience demand, the radio business, including radio news, has remade itself. More plentiful than ever, radio news comes in new packages designed for different audiences.

In the early days, radio was a rather comfortable business; in most markets, a few stations shared a rapidly growing audience, most broad-casting "full service" formats designed to attract listeners from all age and economic groups. Stations worked to build large and loyal audiences, which learned to count on their favorite stations for everything they wanted in content. At most stations, news departments were really departments, employing staffs of reporters to cover local news and produce a variety of public affairs programs. The local news operation usually was augmented by a national network, which provided their local affiliates with large blocks of both news and entertainment programming. In many cases the affiliate relationship was cooperative, with local stations originating news and other programming that the network then could make available to the rest of its affiliates across the country.

Today's radio marketplace is a much different (and a far more dangerous) place. Local stations find themselves fighting harder for smaller audience shares. The average American home has access to five times as many television channels as were available a decade ago, putting even more pressure on an already crowded media market. In larger markets, it is not uncommon for the No. 1 station to enjoy less than a 10 percent audience share, which means nine out of 10 people are listening to something else.

At one end of this increasingly complicated programming spectrum are the all-news stations, which are mostly AMs. The Katz Radio Group says there are 28 all-news stations around the country, plus another 157 stations that program some mixture of news and talk. Over the past decade, the number of stations programming either all-news or news-talk has increased more than 80 percent and the number of all-talk stations has gone up 40 percent. Despite intense competition from music formats, news and talk are not just healthy, but among the fastest-growing formats in radio.

News and information play a crucial role in any radio format, a fact demonstrated quite dramatically during the Persian Gulf war. FM music stations that usually pay little attention to news suddenly discovered that their listeners desperately wanted to know what was happening in the Gulf. Older listeners could count on their regular AM stations to keep them up to date, but Desert Storm was being fought by young men and women from the heart of the FM music demographic, who wanted news from that distant corner of the world that they or their friends might soon be visiting at Uncle Sam's expense. Some music stations, desperate to get war coverage on the air, resorted to stealing the audio from network feeds or CNN's television signal. During the war, radio networks, including CNN's, signed up scores of new stations that never thought they needed a news service.

On the AM side, all-news stations that always enjoy a jump in audience when big news breaks found during the Gulf war that a surprising number of their new listeners came from younger demographic groups, which ran counter to the conventional wisdom that younger listeners had forever abandoned the AM band in favor of rock music in FM stereo. But programmers learned a long time ago that listeners, whatever their age group, don't go looking for formats—they scan the dial until they find what they want. In times of crisis, they want news, even if their usual preference is rock 'n' roll.

In a 1992 Statistical Research Inc. survey, 71 percent of listeners said they probably would stay tuned to news if it came on the station they were listening to, regardless of format. Fewer and fewer stations isolate their news and information programming in conventional newscast blocks, scattering the material throughout the format instead. A 1992 survey conducted for *Radio & Records*, a leading trade publication, found an overwhelming majority of music radio stations continue to program news, even in the face of growing economic pressure to cut back. Many stations said they were, in fact, programming more news than 10 years ago.

The notion that listeners, especially younger listeners, shifted allegiance to FM because of its superior sound quality is largely a myth. While FM listenership has grown steadily over the years, increasing from 28 percent of the total in 1973 to nearly 85 percent in 1993, it is programming, not sound quality, that spawned the migration to the FM band.

In the late 1960s, big AM stations, still clinging to their full-service formats, hesitated to play the new "progressive" music preferred by younger listeners, fearing it might offend the rest of the audience. But small-audience FM stations, with nothing much to lose, eagerly embraced the new music and used it to build a new format characterized by long music sweeps, light commercial loads and carefully targeted news and information. In so doing, they earned the loyalty of the baby-boom generation, the single largest demographic cell ever to move through the population. The rock music formats found all over the FM dial today are direct descendants of those early alternatives. While the dominant AM stations played the same old stuff, the FMs countered with what one consultant calls "music to kill your parents by."

U.S. RADIO FACTS, 1992

Radios in use	576.5 million
Radios sold	71 million
Amount spent on radios	$2.6 billion
Households with radios	96.6 million
Households with portable radios	78%
How many radios per household	5.6 average
Bedrooms with radios	172.3 million
Bathrooms with radios	14.7 million
Cars with radios	95%
Total radio stations	11,338
Commercial AM stations	4,961
Commercial FM stations	4,785
Noncommercial stations	1,592
Americans listen to radio every day	77%
Americans listen to radio every week	96%
Americans with radio at work	61%
Average time listening daily	3 hours, 20 minutes
Total revenues	$8.8 billion
Where adults get morning news	
Newspapers	20%
TV	37%
Radio	38%
None	5%

Source: Radio Advertising Bureau. *Radio Marketing & Fact Book,* 1993.
Bruskin/Goldring Research, 1993; Statistical Research Inc., 1992.

News programming was fashioned especially for that audience as well, news with attitude and information with relevance. The programmers who engineered the FM revolution realized from the start that a successful format had to balance entertainment with news.

As the Gulf war illustrated, listeners expect a radio station, even a music station, to keep them up to date on matters of vital concern. If a station fails to do that, listeners don't hesitate to take their business elsewhere; if the news is important enough, even younger listeners will punch up all-news stations to find the information they need. A music station that is careful to include enough news to satisfy the immediate needs of its listeners is less likely to lose them. Carefully programmed news doesn't drive music listeners away; it actually helps hold them during times of crisis.

News is also the best way for a local station to set itself apart in an increasingly crowded marketplace. Except in the most remote markets where choices may be limited, nobody listens exclusively to one station anymore. The all-news promo line of WINS-AM (1010) in New York, "Give us 22 minutes and we'll give you the world," one of the most successful signatures in radio, concedes up front that listeners are unlikely to stay tuned to the station for very long. In such a confusing and competitive market, a station's local news identity is much more powerful than any music format—Fleetwood Mac and Twisted Sister sound about the same on any frequency, but a package of local news and information is unique and helps a station stand out from its competitors.

Recognizing that listeners are unlikely to stay with the same station every minute, all-news stations try to keep their listeners coming back throughout the day by promising to deliver news, weather, traffic, time checks and other information whenever a listener wants them. Despite much longer listening spans, well-programmed music and talk stations also try to guarantee their listeners the news they want when they want it with the promise that if anything important happens, they will hear about it immediately.

Far from diminishing the quantity or quality of radio news, this intense competition has forced stations to work harder to stake out target audiences and serve particular information needs—just ask those music stations whose audiences evaporated during the Gulf war.

Despite charges of critics that deregulation killed radio news, it is still very much alive. It's true that individual stations can't afford the same range of programming that the old full-service formats routinely delivered, but all the elements of the old format—and a great deal more—are still available somewhere on the dial. There is more information, comment, news and controversy on the radio than ever before, although they may come in different packages targeted at more tightly defined audiences.

In the beginning, the government's role in radio regulation was restricted largely to protecting the reliability of its own wireless communications, primarily between the Navy and its ships at sea. Eventually, however, radio broadcasters themselves sought the government's help to bring order to the increasingly chaotic commercial airwaves. Without some sort of spectrum regulation, anyone could shout but nobody could be heard. That was bad for business, so the businessmen taking over the medium from the scientists and inventors who had developed it embraced government intervention in exchange for economic protection. Unfortunately, these early entrepreneurs were too quick to accept rules that severely limited the use they could make of the radio spectrum by regulating the kinds of programs they could broadcast.

Political considerations—especially the Roosevelt administration's desire to challenge the relentlessly anti-New Deal press establishment—soon came to drive the regulatory process, and from the need to justify politically motivated program-content regulation came the notion that the airwaves are some sort of public trust. Broadcasters accepted this somewhat fuzzy concept as long as the government agreed to shield their monopoly from new competitors. Regulations originally intended merely to organize the spectrum soon evolved into a convenient mechanism to promote the political interests of the president while protecting the exclusive franchises of a relatively small number of incumbent broadcasters. Right from the start, the regulatory process served as much to promote private business interests and powerful political agendas as it did to protect the "public interest" that is still so often cited as the justification for otherwise unconstitutional content regulation.

This public-interest rationale was really just an excuse for government promotion of private business, with the clear understanding, of course, that what those private businesses chose to transmit over the "public" airwaves would never be allowed to offend the personal taste (or political self-interest) of the powerful men in Washington who wrote and enforced the regulations.

On balance, of course, by sheltering the early development of radio, this otherwise unhealthy arrangement did serve the public. But times changed and as the number of competitors in the radio marketplace increased and the explosive growth of television increased the pressure on radio operators accustomed to a comfortable monopoly, the desire for government protection was replaced by a call for regulatory relief. Finally, more than a half-century after the first radio regulations were put in place, the government dropped a number of its programming rules, including the requirement that every station provide a minimum amount of news and information. In a separate development, the courts found that the National Association of Broadcasters (NAB) programming code, to which most stations voluntarily subscribed, violated antitrust laws.

Easing these program-content regulations was reasonable and necessary. After all, where's the "public interest" in forcing a station in Detroit to carry an arbitrary percentage of agricultural programming? The rules had long since degenerated into a bureaucratic numbers game; stations routinely met their content obligations with blocks of low-budget "public affairs" programming on Sunday mornings and network newscasts running automatically through the night. It all counted at license-renewal time, even though few people ever bothered to listen.

From the public's point of view, there was already such an enormous variety of programming available on the dial that the original regulatory purpose had long since been accomplished. By the time the rules were relaxed, they had become little more than a nostalgic reflection of the full-service era. But critics of deregulation angrily accused the government of selling out to the very same business interests those regulations were originally put in place to protect.

In fact, deregulation did not drive news and public-affairs programming off the radio dial. In the years since the rules were changed, surveys conducted for the Radio-Television News Directors Association (RTNDA) have shown clearly that most radio news directors attribute changes in their business almost entirely to economics and market forces, not deregulation. Those same surveys show, moreover, that more than 90 percent of the stations that have chosen to cut back on hard news continue to provide other forms of information and public affairs. A decade after deregulation, separate surveys conducted for RTNDA and the Associated Press show that 80 percent of radio stations still maintain some kind of news operation. In the latest RTNDA survey, only 8 percent of stations that have decided to drop news attribute that decision to deregulation. A small percentage even report that the easing of program-content regulations actually has encouraged them to add more news and public-affairs programming.

Even before deregulation, radio news was undergoing enormous change. By the early 1960s, the traditional radio networks had undergone a complete transformation. For example, the ABC Radio network, recognizing earlier than most the trend toward market fragmentation, split itself into four separate networks to feed news content specifically designed for specialized formats, including rock stations. The national news networks now concentrate on providing affiliates with raw material the stations can use to build locally produced news programs. In many markets, local networks are springing up to feed nonexclusive traffic, weather, sports, business and even hard news programming to several stations at once. Driven by the severe challenges of a fragmenting marketplace, radio programmers continue to take advantage of deregulation to develop new forms of news programming. Mass-market news has been replaced by information carefully targeted to the needs and interests of more narrowly defined demographic groups.

This new way of doing things does not necessarily mean a decline in quality. In 1991, for example, WNSR, a New York rock music station specifically programmed to appeal to young women, took top honors in the RTNDA national awards for a news series on the plight of female Vietnam veterans. This was a story of special interest and importance to the station's target audience, packaged to appeal to those listeners and to be compatible with the station's music format. As this award-winning series illustrates, journalistic quality is not dependent on either the size of an audience or its demographic composition. Indeed, this story about female veterans might never have made it on the air at a station with a less clearly defined target audience.

If, as Marshall McLuhan theorized, radio is a hot medium, then talk radio is undoubtedly its hottest corner. Although talk has been around for years, it was the AMs' desperate search for alternatives to music that has elevated talk to unprecedented popularity and power in recent years.

Consider the now-infamous "tea-bag campaign," in which local talk show hosts around the country whipped their listeners into a frenzy of opposition to a routine congressional pay raise. As the hosts urged their listeners to stage a new Boston Tea Party, congressional offices were

deluged with hundreds of thousands of tea bags, and the pay raise proposal quickly sank out of sight. A single talk show host in Massachu-
setts is credited with the unexpected defeat of a seat belt law there. More
recently, the extraordinary amount of attention on talk shows to President Clinton's proposal to lift the ban on gays in the military pushed the
issue to the top of the national agenda and pressured many members of
Congress to oppose the plan.

Politicians clearly recognize the power and popularity of talk radio;
many have come to fear it. New proposals to bring back content regulations such as the fairness doctrine are motivated, at least in part, by
embarrassing incidents like the tea bag campaign. A medium capable of
mobilizing millions of ordinary people to oppose a congressional pay
raise is a force to be reckoned with and, if at all possible, controlled.

The new king of talk radio, Rush Limbaugh, boasts an audience of 15
million listeners a week. The long-running Larry King is not far behind.
In the last election campaign, candidates fell all over themselves to appear on both shows; Ross Perot chose the Larry King Show to announce
his intention to run for president—twice!

But is what Limbaugh, King and the rest are doing really news? Should
talk shows be considered information or public affairs? Listeners seem
to think so. After all, if a candidate decides to commit news on a talk
show, with questions coming from host and listeners alike, the line between entertainment and public affairs has been crossed. Despite what
more traditional radio newspeople may wish, listeners have made the
choice. The rules have changed and a new kind of news programming
has been born.

Change, of course, is always disconcerting, and critics who yearn for
the good old days of voluntary codes and full-service formats tend to
blame deregulation for everything they hate about modern radio. While
they often characterize program deregulation as an outright sellout to
big business and a shameful abandonment of the public interest, the
hard economic evidence suggests that 50 years of government regulation was far kinder to the economic interests of radio broadcasters than
the more recent decade of deregulation. By encouraging competition
and promoting diversity, deregulation has clearly benefited the genuine
"public interest." With well over half of all commercial radio stations
operating at a loss, the jury is still out on whether deregulation has been
equally beneficial to the radio business. But while radio in general is

struggling, a 1992 RTNDA survey found that only 14 percent of radio news departments were operating at a loss—almost half were delivering a solid profit to their station's bottom line.

In retrospect, deregulation merely ratified long-established patterns of listener demand. The style and structure of radio news had changed long before the government caught up with public preferences and dropped its programming requirements. When the rules did finally change, some news departments that had existed only to satisfy artificial regulatory requirements disappeared. But they were replaced by new forms of news presentation, often unrecognizable to those who grew up with more traditional styles, but very appealing to modern audiences.

As new technologies remake the media landscape, radio news will continue to evolve. Sound, which is processed by the mind in an entirely different (and often more powerful) way than pictures, will continue to play an important role in news presentation. New digital technologies already under development will further enhance radio's ability to gather and deliver vital information rapidly and reliably, and talk radio may well serve as a natural bridge to the interactive media environment of the future.

Whatever form radio news assumes in the future, however, the free market must be allowed to work its will. Just as it is impossible to legislate good taste or sound judgment, it is unwise to allow politicians to define the news or determine how it should be presented. No politician is clever enough to outwit the free market forever, and government intrusion, even a requirement that broadcasters provide something the FCC considers legitimate news, is a threat to liberty and an affront to the Bill of Rights. In the end, broadcasters can be genuinely responsible to the public interest only if the public, not the government, determines how that interest is best served.

David Bartlett is president of the Radio-Television News Directors Association in Washington, D.C.

II

Radio as Cultural Expression

5

The Vocal Minority in U.S. Politics

Andrew Kohut and Carol Bowman

Increasingly in the 1990s, American public opinion is being distorted and exaggerated by the voices that dominate the airwaves of talk radio, respond to call-in polls and clog the White House switchboard every time the administration stumbles.

Rather than genuinely reflect widespread public disquiet, these voices often caricature and exaggerate discontent with American political institutions. Notably, the vocal minority sounds a conservative tone on many issues and is much more critical of President Bill Clinton and his policies, for example, than is the average American. At a time in American politics when active public expression in the form of talk radio, letters to the White House and Congress and newer forms of electronic populism are being venerated, the voices of the vocal few represent a significant advantage for the GOP over the Democratic Party. Republicans have louder voices than Democrats in almost all of the important venues of public expression. As a consequence, Bill Clinton's disapproval score is 10 to 15 percentage points higher among people who have talked on the radio, written their congressional representatives or responded to 1-800 or 1-900 call-in polls than it is in the general population.

A 1993 survey of 1,507 randomly selected Americans by the Times Mirror Center for the People and the Press found that the vocal minority expresses itself in many ways. The study was designed to explore how Americans are making their voices heard in the new electronic age, and to examine the ways in which the distinctive views of the vocal minority differ from those of the rest of the population. There are two methods in particular by which this vocal minority exercises

AMERICANS & TALK RADIO

Have ever listened to talk radio	61%
Listen either "regularly" or "sometimes"	42%
Listened yesterday or today	23%
Listen regularly	17%
Have tried to call in	11%
Have talked on the air	6%
Have talked on-air in the past year	3%
Have talked on-air in the past two months	1%

its clout: talk radio and contacts with congressional offices. We focus here on the first of these.

If contacting your congressional representative is the most activist form of political expression, talk radio represents the widest window on the world of politics and issues for the vocal minority. Almost half of all Americans listen to talk radio on a relatively frequent basis, with one in six listening regularly, Times Mirror's nationwide survey found. Talk radio not only attracts millions of listeners, the poll showed, but millions of them also have either called in to express their views on the air, or aspire to. Eleven percent of the 1,507 U.S. adults surveyed said they had attempted to call into a radio program; 6 percent had gotten on the air. As many as 3 percent of the respondents had called talk shows with their views in the previous 12 months.

In one sense, the talk radio audience looks very much like the nation as a whole in terms of age, sex, race, education and income. In another sense, however, in terms of their politics, those who listen to talk radio are considerably different from the rest of the country: They are more likely to be Republican than the U.S. norm and more likely to be conservative in their political outlook.

There is a slight gender gap among those who say they listen to talk radio either regularly or sometimes—45 percent of men and 38 percent of women. There are few differences by either race or age, although slightly more of those over 30 report listening regularly. And there is a slightly larger socioeconomic gap, with better educated individuals and wealthier households reporting more exposure to talk radio. These dif-

WHO LISTENS TO TALK RADIO

	Regularly	Sometimes	Rarely	Never	DK	N
TOTAL	17%	25%	19%	39%	*=100	(1507)
SEX						
Male	18	27	20	34	*=100	(760)
Female	15	23	18	44	*=100	(747)
RACE						
White	17	24	19	39	*=100	(1292)
Non-White	13	26	18	41	*=100	(210)
AGE						
Under 30	12	28	20	39	*=100	(380)
30–49	17	25	20	37	*=100	(620)
50+	19	22	16	42	1=100	(490)
EDUCATION						
College Grad.	22	24	23	31	*=100	(499)
Other College	17	25	20	27	*=100	(434)
H.S. Grad.	14	25	17	43	1=100	(499)
< H.S. grad.	15	21	14	51	*=100	(122)
FAMILY INCOME						
$50,000+	24	22	21	32	*=100	(339)
$30,000–$49,999	17	27	17	38	*=100	(348)
$20,000–$29,999	16	27	23	33	1=100	(295)
< $20,000.	13	24	16	46	*=100	(411)
REGION						
East	17	20	14	49	*=100	(301)
Midwest	14	23	22	39	1=100	(408)
South	17	26	19	37	*=100	(550)
West	18	29	20	33	*=100	(248)
PARTY ID						
Republican	26	24	18	32	*=100	(434)
Democrat	12	23	19	44	1=100	(490)
Independent	14	27	20	38	*=100	(506)
IDEOLOGY						
Liberal	11	25	19	43	1=100	(203)
Conservative	24	25	20	30	*=100	(381)
In-Between	15	25	19	41	1=100	(871)

ferences, however, are quite modest, ranging only about 9 percentage points from the lowest category in the groupings to the highest.

It is political orientation that yields the largest group differences in talk show listening: Republicans are twice as likely as Democrats to listen regularly to talk radio, 26 percent to 12 percent. Overall, 50 percent of Republicans say they listen to talk radio either regularly or sometimes, compared with 35 percent of Democrats and 41 percent of Independents. The same pattern holds true with ideology: Those who describe themselves as conservatives are twice as likely to be regular listeners as are liberals—24 percent to 11 percent. Half of all conservatives say they listen either regularly or sometimes, compared with 36 percent of liberals and 40 percent of those in between.

Interestingly, while there are no age, gender or racial differences in who *listens* to talk radio, there are differences in terms of who tries to *call in*, with an additional filtering process in terms of who actually makes it onto the air. Men, for example, are far more likely to call than are women, 14 percent to 7 percent, and are almost twice as likely to actually make their views known on the air, 9 percent to 5 percent. While nonwhites (17 percent) are more likely than whites to call—17 percent to 11 percent—there is no difference by race among those who get on the air. While there are modest education and age differences in who listens, those differences are largely muted in terms of who calls radio programs and who actually speaks on the air.

The partisan differences observed in who listens to talk radio are also reflected in the makeup of callers and on-air talkers. Republicans are more likely than Democrats both to call in and to make it onto the air, as are conservatives. Thus, there appears to be both a Republican and conservative tone, or bias, to the voice of public opinion as represented by talk radio. Overall, Republicans and conservatives outnumber Democrats and liberals 2-to-1 over the nation's talk radio airwaves: 8 percent of Republicans have talked on the air, compared to 3 percent of Democrats; 9 percent of conservatives have been on-air, but only 4 percent of liberals.

Both listeners and callers see talk radio as nonideological, presenting a diversity of views rather than being dominated by either liberals or conservatives. Sixty percent believe that talk radio presents a mixture of different views, and 13 percent say talk radio presents no particular point of view. Only 16 percent say talk radio presents a liberal point of view; 11 percent say it is dominated by conservatives.

But although most talk show listeners think the range of views expressed on the air is diverse, they find talk show hosts easier to classify in ideological terms. Examples of Rush Limbaugh aside, one-third of all talk show listeners say "most of the hosts on talk radio" are more liberal than they are, although 19 percent find hosts more conservative than they are. Forty-two percent say talk show hosts either have roughly the same ideology as they do, or that the beliefs and opinions of talk show hosts are widely mixed. While regular listeners and callers differ little from the larger audience of all listeners, there are predictable differences in perceptions of talk show hosts among those with clear partisan or ideological views. More than half—52 percent—of conservative listeners think hosts are more liberal than they are, while just 7 percent say the hosts are more conservative. Liberals offer somewhat of a mirror image—30 percent say hosts are more conservative than they themselves are, and 20 percent say hosts are actually more liberal.

There is no single factor that stands out as talk radio's primary attraction. When asked to identify the most important reason they listen to talk radio, just over one-third (36 percent) mention something having to do with it being a good way to keep up on issues and current events. One in five (21 percent) listens primarily to learn how different people feel about issues of the day and to hear other viewpoints, with another 10 percent offering the related view that they listen to talk radio mainly because it serves as a forum for public opinion. About one in 10 listens to be entertained. No other single reason was mentioned by more than 5 percent of respondents. Surprisingly, only 1 percent volunteered that the most important reason for listening was that they liked a particular host.

We also gave the talk radio listeners a list of six reasons and asked them whether each was a major, minor or "not a reason" why they tune in to the program they listen to most often. More than 70 percent of all listeners (and an even greater proportion of regular listeners and callers) gave surveillance reasons—keeping up on issues of the day and learning how different people feel about different issues—as the major reasons why they listen to talk radio. Another 58 percent gave another information-related reason: that talk radio is a good place to learn things that cannot be learned elsewhere.

Second, in addition to these primary reasons, there are various other appeals of talk radio of lesser importance, but still significant. Some four in 10 of all listeners and half of *regular* listeners cited the entertainment value of talk radio as a major reason they listen. One-third also say they listen to use what they hear on talk radio in discussions of current events with other people. Again, the host ranked at the bottom of the list as a primary appeal—just over one-quarter of all listeners and fewer than 40 percent of regular listeners and callers say the host is a major reason why they listen to the specific talk show they listen to most often.

People who had expressed their views on politics and policy in some way, including those who have talked on the air, differed most from the average U.S. citizen in how they judged the new Clinton administration. In this area, their responses showed that talk show callers are out of sync with general U.S. public opinion, far more critical of Clinton's job performance, far more negative about his economic programs and far more hostile to him personally than the public at large. At the time of the survey, national public opinion was fairly evenly divided on Clinton's overall job performance, with slightly more disapproving of the job he was doing (43 percent) than approving (39 percent). But more than half (53 percent) of radio talk show callers rated Clinton negatively, while 38 percent gave the president a positive grade.

Radio's vocal minority was also more negative about Clinton's economic program than were "average Americans" responding to national surveys. While national opinion of the plan was divided evenly at the time of our survey (42 percent in favor, 41 percent opposed), most of the talk radio participants didn't like the Clinton economic plan (39 percent in favor, 53 percent opposed). There was an even larger disjuncture in opinion about Bill Clinton personally: At the time of the survey, 60 percent of Americans gave Clinton a favorable rating, with 35 percent unfavorable; regular talk listeners were evenly split—48 percent favorable and 48 percent unfavorable.

The vocal minority's views on Bill Clinton may reflect the influence of talk show hosts who conduct the political discourse. As part of this project, the Times Mirror Center also interviewed a representative sample of 112 talk show hosts in major markets and found them extremely critical of Bill Clinton. Just 26 percent of the talk show hosts approved of Clinton's performance and, by a margin of 48 percent to 32 percent, said

WHO CALLS IN TO TALK RADIO

	Ever Called	Ever Talked	N
TOTAL	11%	6%	(1507)
SEX			
Male	14	9	(760)
Female	7	5	(747)
RACE			
White	11	6	(1292)
Non-White	17	7	(210)
AGE			
Under 30	8	2	(380)
30–49	15	7	(620)
50+	10	6	(490)
EDUCATION			
College Grad.	11	7	(499)
Other College	14	6	(434)
H.S. Grad.	10	4	(499)
< H.S. grad.	11	7	(122)
FAMILY INCOME			
$50,000+	12	8	(339)
$30,000–$49,999	13	7	(348)
$20,000–$29,999	13	7	(295)
< $20,000	10	3	(411)
REGION			
East	11	6	(301)
Midwest	10	5	(408)
South	13	7	(550)
West	11	4	(248)
PARTY ID			
Republican	14	8	(434)
Democrat	9	3	(490)
Independent	12	6	(506)
IDEOLOGY			
Liberal	12	4	(203)
Conservative	16	9	(381)
In-Between	10	5	(871)

TALK SHOW HOSTS' PERCEPTIONS OF THE KINDS OF CALLERS WHO ARE "OVER-" AND "UNDER-" REPRESENTED ON THEIR SHOWS

	Over	Under	No Difference	DK
People who are angry	52%	7%	39%	2=100
People who dislike the president	45	8	45	2=100
People who are anti-government	45	8	42	5=100
People who are conservative	50	19	30	1=100
People who dislike Congress	36	5	58	1=100
People who are pro-life	42	11	44	3=100
People who are strongly religious or moralistic	42	20	35	3=100
People who are hostile to gays and lesbians	38	20	41	1=100
Feminists	18	56	23	3=100
People who are liberal	29	50	19	2=100
People who are pro-choice	19	37	44	1=100
People who are racially intolerant	26	30	42	2=100

they expected Clinton to fail rather than succeed in achieving his most important legislative goals.

The negativism of the talk show hosts toward Clinton did not reflect an ideological or partisan bias, however. Talk show hosts are clearly more middle-of-the-road and politically independent than their audiences, despite the prominence of Rush Limbaugh and other conservative talk personalities. The Times Mirror Center's sampling found a slight plurality of hosts leaning to the Democratic Party and a relatively even split between hosts describing themselves as liberal-leaning and conservative-leaning. In fact, 39 percent of this sample said they voted for Clinton, 23 percent for George Bush and 18 percent for Ross Perot.

ATTITUDE DIFFERENCES BETWEEN TALK SHOW HOSTS, REGULAR LISTENERS AND THE GENERAL PUBLIC ON FOUR SOCIAL ISSUES

	Favor	Oppose	Don't Know	N
Proposals to allow gays and lesbians to serve in the military				
Talk Hosts	63%	33%	4%=100	(112)
Regular Listeners	30	63	7=100	(277)
General Public	36	53	10=100	(1507)
A constitutional amendment to permit prayer in the public schools				
Talk Hosts	39	58	3=100	(112)
Regular Listeners	72	24	4=100	(277)
General Public	69	26	5=100	(1507)
Changing the laws to make it more difficult for a women to get an abortion				
Talk Hosts	14	83	3=100	(112)
Regular Listeners	29	62	8=100	(277)
General Public	32	60	8=100	(1507)
Proposals for "term limitations" to limit the number of years that members of Congress can serve				
Talk Hosts	70	28	2=100	(112)
Regular Listeners	77	17	5=100	(277)
General Public	76	18	6=100	(1507)

An overview of the radio talk show hosts interviewed found them to be well educated, affluent and largely independent politically. Most also rejected ideological labels, with 21 percent describing themselves as conservative, 22 percent describing themselves as liberal and most—53 percent—saying they were in between. When the "in-betweens" were asked for their inclinations, 43 percent said they were liberal or liberal-leaning vs. 46 percent conservative or conservative-leaning.

Most hosts feel they play a significant role in shaping public opinion and have an impact on public policy and politics. Although many (25 percent) acknowledge the entertainment value of their programs, more—40 percent—see their job as informing the public; 35 percent volun-

EVALUATIONS OF POLITICAL FIGURES AND INSTITUTIONS BY TALK SHOW HOSTS, REGULAR LISTENERS AND THE GENERAL PUBLIC

	Favorable	Unfavorable	No Opinion	N
Bill Clinton				
Talk Hosts	46%	53%	5%=100	(112)
Regular Listeners	48	48	3=100	(277)
General Public	60	34	1=100	(1507)
Robert Dole				
Talk Hosts	56	42	2=100	(112)
Regular Listeners	60	27	13=100	(277)
General Public	48	28	24=100	(1507)
Ross Perot				
Talk Hosts	39	58	3=100	(112)
Regular Listeners	65	30	5=100	(277)
General Public	64	31	5=100	(1507)
Congress				
Talk Hosts	25	73	2=100	(112)
Regular Listeners	34	59	6=100	(277)
General Public	43	48	9=100	(1507)
The United Nations				
Talk Hosts	62	34	4=100	(112)
Regular Listeners	68	20	12=100	(277)
General Public	73	17	10=100	(1507)
Daily Papers				
Talk Hosts	54	42	4=100	(112)
Regular Listeners	78	18	4=100	(231)
General Public	81	13	6=100	(1235)
Network TV News				
Talk Hosts	54	42	4=100	(112)
Regular Listeners	76	22	4=100	(231)
General Public	81	15	4=100	(1235)
The Supreme Court				
Talk Hosts	86	12	2=100	(112)
Regular Listeners	72	18	10=100	(277)
General Public	73	18	9=100	(1507)
The Church				
Talk Hosts	64	26	10=100	(112)
Regular Listeners	82	12	6=100	(277)
General Public	82	10	8=100	(1507)

teered that their job entails both. Most (63 percent) said they "often play an important role in shaping or influencing public opinion" in their community, and three-quarters were able to recall a case in the recent past when they or something that happened on their show had an impact on public policy or politics. Most of these had to do with bringing a local issue to the forefront. Another 19 percent said local elections had been influenced by something that took place on their show, while another 15 percent thought they had affected public policy by bringing what they believed to be public opinion to the attention of governmental decision makers. About the same number said they had had an impact on politics or policy through pointing out government corruption. In rating the importance of several issues, talk show hosts were far more likely to be concerned about the quality of public education, the general shape of the economy and the federal budget deficit than the general public, but they were less likely than the public to place a high priority on environmental protection, the homeless and the abortion debate.

These talk show hosts expressed more liberal points of view than the public generally and than their audiences specifically. They were far more likely to support allowing gays in the military and to oppose a constitutional amendment to allow prayer in school. They also were slightly more likely to be pro-choice and anti-term limits for members of Congress.

The talk show hosts also were more critical of various institutions than the public, including the Congress, the United Nations, network TV news and the Church. On the other hand, they were more positive than the public about the Supreme Court. The biggest gap between talk show hosts and their public was in regard to Ross Perot. Perot got a 58 percent-to-39 percent unfavorable rating from the hosts, while 65 percent of their regular listeners and 64 percent of all listeners rated Perot favorably. The vocal minority also was more critical of the effectiveness and intrusiveness of government bureaucracy and less supportive of social welfarism than average Americans, and more likely to believe that blacks have made social progress in recent years and to oppose racial quotas. On the other hand, despite these conservative tendencies, the vocal minority was more tolerant and supportive of personal freedoms than less active elements of the public.

Although hosts say the people who call in to their programs represent the public at large, they acknowledge that callers tend to be biased. They describe callers as more likely to be angry, anti-government, more critical of the president and Congress, and by and large more conservative than the average citizen in their communities. Most hosts (52 percent) said "people who are angry" typically were overrepresented on their programs—only 7 percent said angry people were underrepresented—while 39 percent saw no difference in the anger levels of callers and the larger community they come from.

Besides being more angry, talk radio callers are also unrepresentative in that they are more critical than others, according to the hosts. By a wide margin, 45 percent to 8 percent, hosts said people who dislike President Clinton were likely to be overrepresented on their shows, although 45 percent thought the callers' views represented public opinion fairly accurately. The same held true for Congress: 36 percent of hosts thought negative opinions about Congress were overrepresented by their callers, although 58 percent said callers' views were typical of the larger public.

This more negative view of the president and Congress goes beyond specific actors to the political system itself. Hosts characterized their callers as being unrepresentative of the general public in that they expressed a strong anti-government bias. In keeping with this anti-government stance, hosts thought callers were far more conservative in their political orientation than the public as a whole. Half of all hosts interviewed said they thought conservatives were overrepresented by those who call in to their programs; just 19 percent said conservatives were underrepresented. Half also thought liberals were underrepresented among callers.

This conservative tone of public opinion extends to a number of issues and groups, the hosts said. Large pluralities said people who are pro-life tend to be overrepresented, and people who are pro-choice tend to be underrepresented among those who call in. Feminists also are underrepresented among callers, while those who are strongly moralistic or religious, and those who are hostile to gays and lesbians, are likely to be overrepresented on the air.

While talk show hosts acknowledge that their callers are unrepresentative of the general U.S. public, they believe that their callers *are* representative of another important community—their listeners (although not necessarily of all radio listeners in general). An extraordinary 71 percent of hosts described their listeners as "more critical in their views of government and politics than others in their listening area." While a bare majority of hosts (51 percent) said their listeners are representative of the larger community, far more said there is a conservative bias to their audience (34 percent) than feel their listeners are more liberal than the public as a whole (13 percent).

Active and even strident public expression is a measure of a healthy democracy. But given the current political environment and rapid changes in communications technology, it is important to understand who in America speaks out and who does not. This survey offers one yardstick on the partisan, ideological and attitudinal chartacteristics of the vocal minority of radio talk show callers, as compared with the American public at large. What we hear is not necessary what we are.

About the Survey

The results are based on telephone interviews conducted under the direction of Princeton Survey Research Associates among a nationwide sample of 1,507 adults, 18 years of age or older, during the period May 18-24, 1993. For results based on the total sample, one can say with 95 percent confidence that the error attributable to sampling and other random effects is plus or minus 3 percentage points.

The portion dealing with talk show hosts is based on telephone interviews conducted under the direction of Princeton Survey Research Associates among a sample of 112 radio talk show hosts during the period May 25-June 11, 1993. For results based on the total sample, one can say with 95 percent confidence that the error attributable to sampling and other random effects is plus or minus 10 percentage points.

Andrew Kohut is director and Carol Bowman is the research director of the Times Mirror Center for the People & the Press in Washington, D.C.

6

Triumph of the Idol—Rush Limbaugh and a Hot Medium

Tom Lewis

"A man, a legend, a way of life. I am Rush Limbaugh from the Limbaugh Institute for Advanced Conservative Studies. Yes, my friends, the Doctor of Democracy is on the air." So he begins. "Diddle up, Diddle up, Diddle up, bup, bup," he croons. The shuffle of papers is punctuated by thumps, homeless updates, reports on "The REV-er-END Jackson," sounds of trees being felled or animals slaughtered, predictions about the imminent demise of the Clinton administration, denunciations of "feminazis," revelations about excesses of "environmental wackos" and—always—admonitions about tax-and-spend liberals, the failure of the liberal agenda, the failure of Clinton. Then there are the calls on the 800 number, rock bumpers at the heads and tails of segments, commercials for the *Conservative Chronicle* ("It's timely," says Limbaugh. "It's interesting. It's informative. It's educational. It's enlightening. It's educational. Did I say ed-uc-a...It's educational..."); or the *Limbaugh Letter* ("Every month you receive my keenest insights to help you see through this dense liberal fog.... Protect yourself, your friends and family against the Washington liberal agenda....") or the *American Spectator* ("Call now and we'll rush you our free investigative report on Magic Johnson and AIDS along with 12 issues...."). And at the end, the sonorous voice of announcer John Donovan: "You're listening to the EIB Radio Network." EIB. Excellence in Broadcasting. Rush Limbaugh.

It's all Limbaugh, and it all comes out in, well, a rush. The words tumble forth in disarray to form incomplete sentences and muddled paragraphs. Limbaugh opened a recent show by saying he would speak about Bosnia. But then:

> Zbigniew Brzezinski was on "CBS News" this morning. The only reason I know that [thump, thump] is because he kicked me out of my slot. I was supposed to go at 7:17 but they had Harry Smith. Actually when they move you down it means you're more important—they're trying to extend viewership. So they had me at 7:17 scheduled originally but I made it on at 7:35 with Paula Zahn today. Thank her by the way—I had a great time over there. She's, ahh, she at one time was, I would suggest, in the enemy camp. At one time she was [thump, thump] one who failed to see the humor in my feminist comments but that's all been smoothed out now and she and I are great pals [thump, thump, thump]. Had a great time over there. We will—um—talk about Bosnia at length because, ladies and gentlemen....

And on and on. It is hard to punctuate a Rush transcript because it is difficult to know just when Limbaugh pauses. But no matter how garbled his delivery may be, it works with stunning success. To the consternation of most liberal listeners and many in the media.

This is, the host exults, "not just the year of Limbaugh, but instead the *decade* of Limbaugh." For the moment, at least, he is right. "Just when it appeared Rush Limbaugh's radio success was peaking," the March 8, 1993, issue of *Broadcasting & Cable* declared with surprise, "the fall 1992 Arbitron survey showed that his remarkable ratings rise isn't over yet." In late 1992, 571 radio stations carried the "Rush Limbaugh Show," and that number was still climbing six months later, to 591 in April. In Washington, D.C., Limbaugh had a 10 share of the market; in Cleveland, 13; in Pittsburgh, 14; in Houston, 10; and in Hartford, Conn., 14. Limbaugh releases these statistics himself, strutting the latest returns from Arbitron almost daily. Why shouldn't he? In the face of skeptical "experts," Limbaugh has increased his "12+ AQH" (ratings talk for the average number of persons over 12 years of age who listen in an average quarter-hour) from 300,000 when he began in the fall of 1988, to 4 million in mid-1993. He reaches nearly 16 million people each week.

All but five of the nearly 600 stations carrying Limbaugh nationwide are AM, many in serious financial difficulties; several have filed Chapter 11. They receive the program from a satellite and, for most, Limbaugh barters the show, something few in the organization like to acknowledge. "Bartering"—distributing the program to stations free of charge in exchange for a negotiated amount of advertising time—has always been regarded as *infra dig* in the industry. But, in fact, bartering is more common than most want to acknowledge, and both Limbaugh and his stations do very well by it. Limbaugh gets a substantial share of the advertising revenue while the stations get Rush and his high ratings.

Who *are* these people? Sixty-five percent of Limbaugh's listeners are men, a spokesman for the show says, 55 percent age 25 to 54. In addition to being well educated and affluent, the Limbaugh spokesman says, the average Rush listener is "extremely well-read." How well educated? How well-read? Eighty-five percent, the spokesman maintains, have attended at least one year of college. If true, that statistic is surprising, especially as Limbaugh himself frequently pitches ads for something called "Verbal Advantage," ("Achievement Dynamics' powerful vocabulary-building course...gives you the words you need to make your best impression, carefully chosen power words that will give your vocabulary confidence in any situation"), and advertisements are beamed nationally for something called "Hooked on Phonics," a program of audiotapes to teach some of those well-read listeners how to read. ("It's as easy as A-B-C-D-E-F-G.")

Whatever the audience's education, no one disputes its size and its continuing growth. From noon to 3 p.m. Monday through Friday, Limbaugh broadcasts live from New York. In a move reminiscent of the days of "Amos 'n' Andy," when restaurants lured customers with the program, 150 restaurants around the country have opened "Rush Rooms," special sections of their establishments where their luncheon clientele can hear the man, the legend, the way of life.

How did this happen? How is it that a Limbaugh, dismissed early by radio "experts" as a star that would quickly fade from the firmament, now streaks the radio heavens? For the answers to these questions we must turn to politics, history, current radio technology and the persona of Rush Limbaugh himself.

The political reasons, of course, are best known and most cited. Almost all who listen maintain fervently that he speaks the truth as he fulminates daily about militant homosexuals, the excesses of the feminist movement, "wacko" environmentalists, gun controllers, vegetarians or any of the other "liberal" cause-mongers who exasperate him. Limbaugh's partisans listen with the rapt adoration usually reserved for a lover or a divinity. Almost all the calls he takes from listeners—about a dozen each program—are prefaced with "dittos," the Limbaugh idolizer's shorthand for "How do I love thee?" ("Double dittos from the Music City," begins Al from Nashville. "Conservative atheist dittos from the home of David Duke, who has followed your footsteps into talk radio," says a caller from Louisiana.) Many would support him for president. Women want to bear his child. From Diane in Memphis: "Let's talk about something more pleasant, like having babies like 'Rush Limbaugh the fourth.'")

Many conservatives contend that it's Limbaugh's political message that accounts for his popularity, but that is clearly not the case; other conservatives—G. Gordon Liddy and David Duke for example—articulate conservative themes but are comparatively unloved. Limbaugh's success speaks more to the power of radio and his ability to use the medium; he is a creature of the medium in which he has long worked. Better than most liberals or conservatives, he's a consummate showman who understands radio and sound, especially their ability to create a picture in the minds of listeners and their potential to capture imaginations.

For all we hear today about Rush Limbaugh's phenomenal success, few remember that it does have its antecedents. He has revived—perhaps perfected—the art of using radio to connect, an art that most in the business seemingly have forgotten. Consciously or not (I suspect the latter), Limbaugh draws upon a tradition that includes figures as diverse as Dr. Brinkley, Huey Long, Father Coughlin, Jack Benny, Fred Allen and even the Great Gildersleeve. Undoubtedly, the message of these forerunners was different, but their methods bear striking similarities.

Broadcasting in the 1920s and early '30s over station KFKB ("Kansas Folks Know Best") in Milford, Kan., Dr. John Romulus Brinkley delivered lectures three times a day about the virtues of implanting goat glands in men to restore their potency.

"You people who are all the time grunting and groaning, never fit for anything, you are entirely to blame for your condition," Dr. Brinkley proclaimed. Patients by the thousands boarded the trains to Milford, checked themselves into the "Brinkley Hospital" and selected a goat from a pen adjacent to the operating room for their rejuvenation. In the late 1920s, Brinkley broadcast "The Medical Question Box," a show that featured the doctor reading letters from listeners ($2 each) and prescribing his own specially concocted medicines at $1 a bottle. In the 1930s, with his radio programs under siege by federal and medical authorities, Brinkley turned to politics, running a close third in the race for governor of Kansas in 1932.

From Baton Rouge, Huey Long raged against "lyin' newspapers," promised "every man a king" and complained that though the Lord had invited the world to a feast, "Morgan and Rockefeller and Mellon and Baruch have walked up and took 85 percent of the vittles off the table." Long, first as governor and then U.S. senator, borrowed some of the goat-gland doctor's tactics to appeal to Louisianians over the radio, taking to the medium almost instantly and understanding its power better than most. In 1933, seeking national office, the "Kingfish" bought time on NBC to broadcast his message of "share our wealth" across the country. Other national broadcasts followed and his popularity seemed to grow each time; in the first three months of 1935, Long spoke six times to huge audiences, who sent as many as 60,000 letters to the network and thousands more directly to Baton Rouge. Share Our Wealth Clubs sprang up in many communities and states.

Beginning in 1926, Father Charles Coughlin, a priest from the Detroit suburb of Royal Oak, delivered weekly talks over Detroit's WJR. At first, Coughlin confined his remarks to religion and morals, giving his speeches such lofty titles as "The Importance of Religion in a Man's Life," but as his popularity grew and the boom of the 1920s crashed into the Depression, he turned to vigorous denunciations of bolshevism and socialism and the fast approaching "Red Menace." In the spring of 1931, he purchased time from William Paley's Columbia Broadcasting System so that he might disseminate his message across the nation. Soon, he required 100 clerks simply to answer his mail and organized his listeners into the "National Union for Social Justice" and the "Radio League of the Little Flower." When the CBS station in Philadelphia asked listeners if they would prefer Coughlin or the New York Philharmonic on Sunday afternoons, Coughlin won, 187,000 to 12,000. But each week Coughlin gradually became more venomous. The "Red Menace" gave way to "international bankers," a term that insinuated anti-Semitism. These bankers, Coughlin contended, had caused listeners to lose their jobs and their families to starve in the worst depression the country had ever known. "Democracy is over," the radio priest declared darkly. Paley canceled the program.

Brinkley, Long and Coughlin shared this: Each had a single message and portrayed himself as being on the outside, oppressed in one way or another by government or established interests. Brinkley, the goat-gland doctor, railed against federal authorities and the "psycho-bunko" of the Kansas State Medical Board's "jealous oligarchs." His candidacy for governor, under the banner "Let's Pasture the Goats on the Statehouse Lawn," was as much a maneuver to continue selling his medicines and operations as an attempt to take over the capitol. Long took on Standard Oil in Louisiana, then the forces of corruption in Baton Rouge (substituting his own in the process) and, finally, Franklin D. Roosevelt. Coughlin, especially at his peak in the mid-1930s, ranted about communists and Jews, who, he convinced himself, had financed the Russian Revolution. Weren't Hitler and Nazi Germany, reasoned the priest with his confused and twisted logic, preferable to Jews and Communist Russia?

Each of these Limbaugh predecessors had an engaging, almost conspiratorial, way of bringing his audience into league with him. Each gave the listener the sense that, together, they were right-thinking people who would create a better world. Limbaugh's tone is equally conspiratorial, urging listeners, "It's time to stop feeling like you're the minority because you are a traditional American. It's just time to stop feeling you're in the minority [thump shuffle thump], 'cause you're not."

Nor do the similarities end with the method of delivery; they extend to the audience itself. There are niches on radio, particularly AM, that have always appealed to those who feel themselves excluded from the political mainstream, who think they've been forced to the economic and social margins of American life by the country's dominant political powers. In the 1930s, old-line populists said that they had no jobs, their families were starving and they had been forgotten by the rich and powerful. Today, they say that they don't have the advantage of a college education, don't have the special privileges reserved by government for minorities and the rich, don't have the jobs that promise real advancement—they are the forgotten. These, the inheritors of the classic populist tradition, are the listeners at whom "Hooked on Phonics" and "Verbal Advantage" tapes are pitched. The *Washington Post*'s Jonathan Yardley calls them "marginal Americans." On the air, they bristle with discontent and resentment.

Limbaugh's instincts are more benign than Long's or Coughlin's, but he has gone one step beyond those predecessors to tap another new reservoir of civic unhappiness. These we may call the new populists, white-collar workers watching the tide of America's greatness recede. Often college-educated, they are the "extremely well-read" members of the Limbaugh audience. Their parents were secure in the knowledge that America was the greatest land of all and they had the houses, cars, jobs and standard of living to prove it. Today, these disillusioned sons and daughters find they must work two jobs just to drive smaller cars and live in overpriced apartments. The stability of their youth is a fading memory. Jobs are no longer secure; marriages are crumbling; violence is unfettered; and people who have long lived on America's margins—homosexuals, blacks, women who desire something other than heterosexual marriage—now get government help and preferential treatment to move into the mainstream. *Their* mainstream.

Like Long and Coughlin before him, Limbaugh articulates the frustrations of these people far better than they could themselves, offering solutions based on his own version of common sense. Limbaugh sounds a single message: Liberals are ruining the country and if we don't stop them, the United States will slide inevitably into fiscal and moral decay. They are bad, bad, bad. Liberals are intolerant, he says—"The mean-spiritedness in this country comes from the left and not from the right." When he isn't berating liberals in preachy harangues filled with "carefully chosen power words," he reads newspaper clippings that record their failures and excesses.

And the Rush Faithful respond with ecstatic shouts of "Ditto!" reminiscent of the way teen-agers shout at the concerts of rock idols. They wear officially licensed "Ditto Head" t-shirts and lapel pins and drink their coffee and tea from Rush Limbaugh "Ditto" mugs. To the bluster, Limbaugh has added humor, mean-spirited, perhaps, but a hot new commodity in either conservative or liberal thought (as a few old issues of the *National Review* and *The Nation* amply illustrate). Limbaugh has drawn from the rich tradition of radio humor—people like Jack Benny, Fred Allen and the Great Gildersleeve—to inject a little life into some tired subjects. Much of the humor seems forced to occasional listeners, but to conservatives it ranks as great satire. When Limbaugh talks about abortion, the sound of a vacuum cleaner comes on in the background, or a spot offers "feminazi" trading cards, each with vital statistics including how many abortions the woman has had. Then there are songs—about the Kennedys' alleged marital infidelities and lyrics about the "big banana"—like this excerpt from a two-minute, mildly thumping rock song echoing a Billy Joel tune:

Bill Clinton is a liar.
Now we see he's yearning to take all we're earning.
Bill Clinton is a liar.
If you got money, hide it 'cause he's gonna find it.

Waco, Reno, Inferno—
She didn't start the fire.
On the job she's learning, while the cult is burning.
When Clinton saw the fire,
Right away he knew it, once again he blew it.

IBM and GM, economy slips again.
New Figures, new facts, lower spending, higher tax.
Health care, spending cuts, economic blood and guts,
Taxes for the middle class, Clinton blow it out your sax.
Refugees with HIV, rented vans, TNT,
Haitians immigrate, they are shark bait,
New men in Marines, hairdressers, closet queens....

"One of the chief pretenders to the throne of God," E. B. White observed more than half a century ago, "is radio itself." The medium, White said then, had "acquired a sort of omniscience..., a pervading and somewhat godlike presence which has come into lives and homes." Today, Rush Limbaugh ("with talent on loan from God, serving humanity simply by opening my mouth") is the most powerful voice on talk radio, for some, a godlike presence.

Conservatives are ecstatic. To many, Limbaugh seems their one bright and shining hope. Liberals are worried. "God forbid that he run for high office," one said to me recently. I told him not to worry—I suspect that Limbaugh himself realizes he is the wizard behind the curtain. The quiet walls of a studio let him create a fiction that seldom stands up to reality, on the street or the campaign trail.

Of greater concern than a Limbaugh should be the idea of the talk show itself. Radio talk shows first were local in nature and served to extend neighborliness. People would phone in to exchange a recipe, report a cat up a tree, talk about a local political issue or announce a bake sale. Some called just to connect with the host. Then in the 1960s, a new era of talk shows began. More aggressive and strident, politics and sex proved to be the best draws, and the safer of the two topics won out. When technology—especially satellites and 1-800 telephone numbers—allowed local talk shows to go national, politicians took to calling in. After he announced his presidential candidacy (twice) on talk TV with Larry King in 1992, Ross Perot was a talk show regular. During the 1992 presidential campaign, candidate Clinton was appearing on local and national talk shows morning, noon and night. President Bush first dismissed the idea as undignified, but before the campaign was over, he, too, had slipped to Rush Limbaugh.

Now no network seems complete without a talk show. Even the august National Public Radio has put a host in a studio equipped with a 1-800 line to serve up an "intelligent" talk program. Across the nation, scores of Limbaugh wannabes sit in radio studios, answer the phones and dream of the big time. New York! Syndication! T-shirts! A book on the best-seller list! Who knows, even a call from the president! Caught in local Arbitron race for market share, these Rush clones dedicate themselves to bringing out the darker angels of their listeners' nature by taking hot stories and heating them up even further. When President Clinton moved early in his administration to fulfill a campaign promise and lift the ban on homosexuals in the military, talk show hosts whipped their audiences into a frenzy. Calls flooded an overworked White House switchboard. "This isn't a government by talk show," complained one member of the administration, forgetting that his boss had done more than any politician to make it just that.

As one particularly astute commentator observed, with an increase in the speed of information comes a decrease in its substance. Talk shows take the trivial and make it substantial. Homosexuals serving in the military is of little consequence when compared with $200 billion deficits and a $4 trillion debt. Yet the lunchtime diner sitting entranced in a Rush Room, or a trucker heading west out of Amarillo on Interstate 40, or a mother sitting in her kitchen in Rapid City, sipping coffee from her Limbaugh mug, hears little of substance about the debt. What does filter through comes in the form of a slogan meant to illustrate the failures of the current administration and its bankrupt liberal agenda.

Talk shows—especially Limbaugh's—have triumphed. Some even credit talk with the unthinkable—saving AM radio. But irksome questions remain: Is our "Doctor of Democracy" really serving us? Does his success signal a triumph for our free expression? Is this glut of hot air really our victory in electronic democracy, or should we, like Pyrrhus, say, "Another victory like that and we're done for"?

Tom Lewis, professor of English at Skidmore College in Saratoga Springs, N.Y., is author of Empire of the Air: The Men Who Made Radio.

7

Talking Over America's Electronic Backyard Fence

Diane Rehm

Talk shows, frequently cited as contributing to the form and outcome of the 1992 presidential campaign, influence not just politics, but society. And that influence is growing. In the "old days," Americans used to talk about issues over the backyard fence, but now talk shows have expanded the back yard. In many ways, both in presidential campaigns and in day-to-day life, the importance of talk radio has been both underestimated and exaggerated.

I've been hosting a daily call-in show in the Washington metropolitan area since 1979, a two-hour program that, like other talk shows, offers callers an opportunity to talk to experts and each other about everything from the latest round of fighting in Bosnia to Middle East peace talks, gays in the military or the Clinton administration's health care program. Arbitron says nearly 100,000 people tune in. Those listeners represent every political stripe from dyed-in-the-wool Reagan Republicans to mainstream moderates to the darlings of the left—and everyone in between. Some talk shows attract particular groups; mine seems to attract all kinds, which enriches the exchange for participants and listeners alike. As host, I've listened with interest over the years to the changing tone of callers. The style and substance of their comments have evolved from halting, sometimes inarticulate groping in the early years to ease with challenging guests and, at times, articulate and authoritative arguments.

In offering a forum for ideas and the exchange of viewpoints, talk radio contributes to a growing understanding of the complex issues confronting the society. It is, perhaps, the epitome of participatory democracy in the electronic age. Sometimes listeners' thoughts and reactions are more on target than those of political leaders and journalists, who are learning to listen to the voices over the electronic backyard fence. Talk-radio listeners alone don't make policy, of course (or sink presidential nominations—Zoë Baird's, for example), but the talk show mike does provide a forum for public opinion that no one in the administration, Congress or the news media can miss. When events get them riled, concerned people call radio shows like mine, and many further express their unhappiness by calling and writing the White House and congressional offices. Then, when listeners hear others voice their opinions, they feel justified in voicing their own. Sometimes the *vox populi* chorus becomes too loud for the wise to ignore, ultimately rising above the din of conventional wisdom.

One example of conventional wisdom is that people who listen to call-in shows are on the fringe, out there, "Americans on the margin," as Jonathan Yardley of the *Washington Post* dismissed them, "people who have an excessive liking for the sound of their own voices, people with too much time on their hands."

That's not my view. Every day I hear from someone who identifies herself or himself as a "long-time listener but first-time caller." Shy, fumbling, quavering at first, they quickly gain strength, adding their voices to what I see as a growing number of thoughtful, concerned citizens who are ready to speak to the issues at hand and eager for their views to be heard. It is this facet of individual empowerment that I believe is generating new excitement about talk radio.

Not long ago I interviewed Diane Eyer, a professor of psychology from the University of Pennsylvania, about what she called the "scientific myth" of mother-infant bonding. Her work focused on previous research that had concluded that healthy mother-child relationships depend on mothers and infants being physically close immediately after birth. Some pediatricians recommended as much as a full year for adequate bonding. Though most of the scientific community has now dismissed this theory as groundless, women continue to be told that the need to bond is so critical that they should not go back to work after having a baby. The theory has substantial social and political ramifications.

That program prompted scores of calls from men and women who had always accepted the bonding theory. Given the opportunity to hear a different view and to question Professor Eyer's conclusions, listeners expressed a collective sense of revelation and relief to hear another side. When researchers come up with prescriptions for living, talk shows are a useful testing ground for differing ideas and views.

In Spring 1993, *Atlantic* magazine published a cover story by Chandler Burr, "Homosexuality and Biology," which examined the biological inquiry into sexual orientation. Shortly after the article came out, Burr was a guest on my program, along with Kenneth Adelman, a self-described conservative nationally syndicated columnist who has long opposed fully integrating gays into the military. After reading Burr's *Atlantic* piece, however, Adelman had written in the *Washington Times* that if sexual orientation was found to be something neither chosen nor changeable, he would have to re-examine his views. As the two debated whether sufficient scientific proof existed to show that homosexuality is immutable, listeners heard two honest men struggling to understand each other's views. In the process, I believe, they helped listeners expand their own capacity to tolerate opinions they might not hold. One caller, who identified himself as gay, challenged Adelman to do some "down-to-earth grassroots research, to talk with gays about how and when they knew they were different." By the end of the program, neither Burr nor Adelman was ready to say he had changed his mind, but there was a feeling that because views had been fairly presented and exchanged, new understanding might emerge.

In late April 1993, as the Clinton administration agonized over whether U.S. military action would be needed in Bosnia, Secretary of State Warren Christopher said public support would be crucial for any change in policy. So I put the question to listeners, and the phone lines were jammed. "Immediate air strikes," said some. Others disagreed: "A European problem not worth the loss of U.S. lives," they said. Some cited the recent opening of the Holocaust Museum in Washington as a reminder of what happens when the world turns its back on events. No, another disagreed, blaming the Bush administration's lack of action more than a year before; the bloodshed could have been prevented *then*. After an hour, the calls were divided about evenly between those favoring unilateral U.S. action and those arguing for no action without United Nations and European support. Beyond the specific question of Bosnia, however, many callers observed that what was most important was the public debate, not just on my talk show in Washington, but across the country.

These days, Americans can choose among many styles and political perspectives in call-in shows and hosts, and listeners tend to tune in where their own views are reflected. In that sense, perhaps the most difficult task facing any talk show host is to remain open to all voices, whatever his own political perspective (I use that male pronoun because there are relatively few female talk show hosts around the country). Sometimes it's tough. I understand the protests of "bias" and "unfairness" leveled at talk hosts. We control the conversation and I believe we're obliged to make our programs a neutral forum for the fair and safe exchange of ideas, whether we agree with them all or not.

Listener safety is critical for talk radio to work. Callers can remain anonymous, sometimes using fictitious "handles." They impart their very personal stories to strangers out in the ether, weep over their losses and express their hopes and their fears. They scream at what they perceive as injustice. For them, when they're talking with me over the phone (and through the airwaves), I am their friend and confidante, someone with whom they can risk a new idea or an unguarded emotion.

But talk radio is also a provocative and even dangerous medium, capable of representing an extreme form of democracy that gives voice and weight to every idea without stifling or censoring. Sharing their thoughts strengthens people in their beliefs. Of course, there will always be some who attempt to use talk shows to spread their own political or social dogma, but these are pretty easily identifiable. Hosts and other listeners are quick to challenge them, tipped off by jargon and buzzwords that are clearly neither spontaneous nor genuine.

At least 40 percent of our listeners hear "The Diane Rehm Show" from their offices, representing a dramatic shift for the population and for talk radio. Twenty years ago, most listeners to a morning show such as mine were women, most often at home. But now, research tells us that both men and women tune in in relatively equal numbers from the workplace. Of course, many women still work at home, caring for their children, and there are many men and women who telecommute, whose professional life also is in the home. Doctors, attorneys, government officials, scientists and journalists call in. So do artists, fishermen, farmers and taxi drivers. Some of these listeners spend much of their time alone or in traffic, so talk radio becomes a lifeline to the rest of the world.

Where Americans from Long Island, N.Y., to Billings, Mont., to San Diego, Calif., once exchanged views and formed opinions by talking with neighbors over backyard fences and when they met on the street, today, talk shows fill that function. We've become far more polarized as a society, more outspoken about our views and even our prejudices, with a greater awareness of the social divides among people. Over the air—if no longer over the fence—talk shows expose and occasionally bridge those differences.

Increasingly, I hear two frequent criticisms of talk radio. First, that listeners are extremists of one stripe or another and, second, that legislators make decisions based on the loudest segments of the population who can monopolize the airwaves. I believe both those concerns are unfounded. My own experience tells me that the public's voice of reason is far better represented on talk radio than the voice of extremism. Given the wide range of opinions on any given subject, people can sort through conflicting ideas and find a way to make sense of the most complicated issues. There will always be polarizing voices and distortions offered as "fact," but given the fragmentation of the U.S. population, what I hear on the phone lines is probably fairly representative of the general population.

Despite the recent flurry of attention to talk shows and their role in national politics, let me say that concerns about megalomaniacal talk show hosts galvanizing their troops to affect policy unfairly are exaggerated. Politicians have many sources of feedback from constituents; views expressed on the air are taken into account—and should be—but they're just one element of the overall picture. Elected officials make the hard decisions after they've read, debated and reflected. For them, sometimes insulated inside the beltway in Washington, D.C., or in state capitol offices in Bismarck, N.D., or Baton Rouge, La., talk shows can provide an early gauge of opinion on tough issues and an accurate reading of what the folks back home are saying over the backyard fence.

Diane Rehm hosts "The Diane Rehm Show" on WAMU-FM in Washington, D.C., an affiliate of National Public Radio.

8

You Are What You Hear

Adam Clayton Powell III

Radio is the audio analogy of the adage "You are what you eat." Just as our physical bodies are a sum of meals we have eaten, our minds are an amalgam of what we have heard, read and thought.

Radio is powerful. Its role in our lives—and in our society—is a function of what it is, what it does, what it can do and what we do with it. Television and movies may expose us to new experiences in specific detail, but radio and literature are unique in engaging the imagination, permitting us to create our own images in the mind's eye. Drama, dance and painting are evocative, but radio, along with the printed word, forces us to collaborate with the medium as an active participant.

As a result, the pictures are better on radio: What you can imagine is almost always scarier, funnier, more real and more vivid than the explicit images of video and film.

Think of the sound of a wave crashing against the shoreline, or of a man gasping for breath in the thin air of Mount Everest. Or hear the Martians' spaceship hatch scraping open in Orson Welles' famous 1938 "War of the Worlds" broadcast. So many and so powerful were the pictures formed in the minds of listeners hearing "news reports" of Martians landing in New Jersey that hundreds panicked, armed themselves, gathered their families and prepared to be vaporized by death rays. Now *those* are pictures.

Video directors learned that lesson: In horror movies, it's a mistake to show the monster before the end of the film. Left to the imagination, our minds create demons far scarier than any filmmaker's image.

Radio is cheap. This powerful instrument is so inexpensive that we often forget it's there. The cost of a radio receiver is almost negligible these days, affordable even in impoverished corners of America and throughout the world.

What goes on radio is also cheap to create and to transmit, especially compared to television. Although camcorders are getting smaller and less expensive every year, video cannot compare with the simplicity and flexibility of sound.

And radio is ubiquitous—powerful, inexpensive tools that have spread to all corners of our lives and everywhere on the globe. Consider the lever and the wheel and how they changed people's lives; now, radio. It's everywhere. We wake up with radio, shower with it, drive with it, eat with it, walk with it, go into space with it, work with it, wait on "hold" with it, play with it and fall asleep with it. We even hear it in elevators. (Yes, Muzak is radio.)

With the possible exception of scuba diving, just about anything we do can be done listening to radio. And is.

Radio is diverse. Most Americans have dozens of choices of radio stations, with more on the way. In addition to new AM and FM stations, we can get radio by cable and soon by direct broadcast satellite.

In most towns, there are scores of music formats and at least three or four news and information services on the air. Some stations emphasize the music, others the information, some both. Others highlight personalities from Paul Harvey to Rush Limbaugh, Garrison Keillor to Howard Stern to Casey Kasem.

Noncommercial stations try programs that do not appeal to larger audiences, such as international music and poetry, as well as programs that do, such as news and classical music.

Television still needs mass audiences, but on radio, as in print, if 10,000 or 20,000 people want it, a station somewhere on the dial probably has it.

Radio is fragmented. There are so many choices on radio that, as in print, listeners may share few common experiences.

Even the best-known programs attract a small sliver of the national audience. Talkmeister supreme Larry King may be on more than 400 stations, but on any given day his radio audience amounts to less than one-half of 1 percent of the population. (In early 1993, King drew just over a million listeners to his late-night show, reported Westwood One, the radio network that carries the program. In February, he moved to afternoons, where the potential audience is larger but where competition also is greater.)

Radio mirrors our own fragmentation: Just as we live and work in largely separate social segments, we listen to self-selected and largely separate segments of radio.

In other words, you are what you hear and you are what you *choose* to hear.

Each radio station tailors itself to a specific target audience, aiming to attract a specific group of people at a particular part of their day. Thus, a station might gather self-selected groups of 1970s soft-rock listeners or jazz devotees or talk radio regulars.

Demographers know who you are if they know where you live. With equal certainty, marketers know who you are if they know which radio stations you listen to. If you are a woman in your early 30s, marketers expect you will choose one of the soft-rock or country music stations. If you are a student in your late teens, you may well spend part of your day with a college or rock station, listening to music people over 25 find completely alien, at least for now. If you are a man over 50, marketers know you listen to a lot of AM for all-news and big band, and to classical music on FM. Opera seems to attract those over 65 (advertisers know that—there aren't many Nike ads on classical music stations).

Radio is community.

Long ago, we gathered around the community fire. Now we gather around our different communities of ether, via radio. But this goes beyond the business of advertisers and marketers. This goes to the heart of identity and community, unbound by geography.

Successful radio stations offer their listeners more than just particular types of music or talk or well-presented news—they also offer shared identity and community.

Radio as community may be especially strong during an emergency, as South Florida residents found when Hurricane Andrew hit and government relief workers distributed tens of thousands of transistor radios to residents who lacked essentials—food, water, electrical power and information. But it does not require a disaster; all it takes is music that appeals to a community of twentysomethings or a call-in program for seniors on fixed incomes or a pair of brothers doing comedy and, almost incidentally, giving advice about carburetors, transmissions and your father's Buick to callers from Bozeman to Boston.

Think of how often you've heard someone—a friend, a spouse, someone on the bus—mention something they heard on the radio. Or how often you have—jokes, music, news, gossip, opinions, even advertising.

Every morning, Howard Stern gives his listeners much to talk about later in the day. Some hate him, but he is a hit because he creates a well-defined community.

In other words, you are what you hear and you hear what you *choose* to be.

America is so big that it has large communities most of us don't know well and other communities most of us don't know at all.

Few readers of this book will ever listen to KLAX-FM in Los Angeles, because it is a local Spanish-language station; most, perhaps, have never heard of it—KLAX is a different community. But it is also the most popular radio station in southern California. From its large and rapidly increasing audience, we know that KLAX has made itself crucial to its community. And KLAX is only one of eight Spanish-language stations in Los Angeles.

The Korean community in Los Angeles has its own Korean-language radio station, which seldom appears in radio and TV listings in Los Angeles newspapers.(Not only doesn't it appear in the program listings, but it is rarely even listed as a station.) Listeners need special radios to receive the signal, a "sideband," and selling those special radios has become a lucrative business in Korean neighborhoods (shades of David Sarnoff's original "radio music box" scheme).

There are some gaps in radio, communities of people that still do not have service. One obvious example is children. True, there are and have been some attempts to serve those not measured by the ratings services' "age 12 and over" category. But radio has yet to produce a Charles Osgood for children or an audio equivalent of Big Bird or Mister Rogers. Perhaps we need a Children's *Radio* Workshop.

There are some efforts to serve that young community, such as the Minneapolis-based Children's Satellite Network, but commercial stations have struggled when they tried to attract an audience of children. And public radio stations usually find children's programs do not "pledge well" (i.e., attract donations from listeners), so few are likely to replace profitable news and music programming for any new children's shows.

And where are the leading women on radio? Not the co-hosts, not the newscasters, but the breakout, crossover, punch-through-the-clutter superstars of the air. Women listeners are highly prized by advertisers, so where is the radio Roseanne, the Oprah of audio? For that matter, there is no minority star either, no network radio counterpart of Bill Cosby, Ed Bradley or the Fresh Prince.

Then there is community radio. Remember the central role of the local station in Spike Lee's movie, "Do the Right Thing"? It was radio devoted to and defined by its community, in that case an urban neighborhood in Brooklyn.

Sure, there are real-life inner-city community stations: Harlem's WLIB-AM is a well known advertiser-supported station, but its appeal crosses geographical boundaries well beyond Harlem. A better example is KPOO-FM, "poor people's radio," in San Francisco's Mission District, which broadcasts avant garde music and talk shows to its urban neighborhood audience.

If inner-city neighborhoods can be isolated by poverty, then for rural areas isolated by distance (and poverty), a local radio station can be a lifeline. The fictitious station in television's "Northern Exposure" is based on life at rural public stations in Alaska. Towns and villages there are so remote that residents may only be able to receive one local signal, their community station, linked by satellite to major cities and "the lower 48" for news of the outside world.

Whitesburg, Kentucky, is isolated by rugged terrain rather than by distance. From Whitesburg, WMMT-FM broadcasts to an isolated, impoverished rural community at the junction of four states, bringing news from around the world and from the local town hall. Because of the rugged mountains, residents cannot easily travel to town meetings, so the station features broadcasts of local discussions at the VFW, news of visitors traveling through the area and local bluegrass music programs from a live remote microphone at the general store. They don't have *that* in Cicely, Alaska.

What community radio does best is what all of radio does best— extend a community to itself. Listeners to WMMT or to Larry King or to the BBC World Service have all elected to become part of that station's community, to join its family of listeners and to engage their imaginations to create that community of spirit in their own minds.

In other words, you are what you hear and, through radio, you hear what you are.

Adam Clayton Powell III, director for technology studies at The Freedom Forum Media Studies Center and a producer for Quincy Jones Entertainment, is former vice president for news and information at National Public Radio.

9

Ear on America

Al Stavitsky

At the end of the 20th century, radio in America is the electronic version of the Founding Fathers' vision of the free and open marketplace of expression as the foundation of democracy. Then, as now, the quality of the message in the public market sometimes may be suspect, but its variety is proof of its vitality.

Think about it: There are 11,338 radio stations in the United States, playing roughly 40 different kinds of music from classic Bach and classic rock, country and hip-hop and rap, to stuff called "heavy metal" and "oldies" and "mellow," "lite" and "new wave." Then there's news, talk, sports, psychic counseling, politics (left wing, right wing, wingless), thoughtful, thoughtless, accordian-polka, fishing tips and car repair.

Value judgments aside, these thousands of radio stations offer some of the most diverse and solid evidence that exists of the value and robust health of free expression. It is also some of the most bizarre, off-putting, rhythmic, compelling, insightful, mindless, interesting, confusing, inept, polished, worthy, well-meaning, maddening and earsplitting stuff ever extended via media from sender to receiver.

But there are fears that new technological, economic and regulatory developments might reduce that diversity of electronic voices. Factors such as satellite services, trafficking in stations and budget cutting have fostered the kind of homogeneity in radio that is anathema to the original concept of diverse expression. Critics worry that when stations sound alike, radio's creativity and excitement may be lost. But spin the dial awhile and you can still find something different, distinctive programming that cuts through the static, easily distinguishable from the other "noise."

Here are just a few examples of dial-spinning, evidence of the diversity, breadth, quality and quirkiness of radio that serve all kinds of Americans every day. These eight stations from eight states across the county, drawn from AM and FM, commercial and public radio outlets—representative only in their dissimilarity—illustrate the idiosyncracies, vitality, problems, depth and dedication of radio. It is a technology that is old in broadcast terms, perhaps, but definitely not passé—in the America of the 1990s. These case studies also highlight the day-to-day value of radio, that "electronic wallpaper" that nearly all Americans make part of their lives.

KBRW—On Top of the World

The KBRW signal kicks out from Barrow across the frozen tundra of Alaska's North Slope Borough, a political subdivision the size of Minnesota that lies within the Arctic Circle and includes Prudhoe Bay, origin of the Alaska Pipeline. No offense to "Northern Exposure," but this is *real* bush radio.

Fewer than 8,000 people live in this harsh land of remote native villages, shimmering northern lights and polar bears on the ice packs. Inaccessible except by air (or foot), North Slope communities are linked 24 hours a day via the region's only local broadcast service—"Top of the World Radio"—and hear eclectic, multilingual programming ranging from Eskimo dancing to Little League basketball to personal messages for people in the bush.

On the air since 1974, KBRW-AM (680) is a public radio station based in Barrow, a city of 3,500 that is the North Slope's economic and political hub. The station is owned and operated by a community group, Silakkuagvik (Inupiat for "communicating through the air") Communications, with a board of directors controlled by Alaska natives. To cover a 90,000-square-mile service area, KBRW operates a 10,000-watt main transmitter with five translators planted in Inupiat villages.

Programming is broadcast in three languages: English, Inupiat Eskimo (spoken by more than 70 percent of the borough's residents) and Tagalog, the native language of the Barrow area's Filipino community. The format is heavy in news and public affairs. Barrow government meetings go out live as a service to listeners in villages up to 300 miles away. Then there are Eskimo stories and legends, Inupiat literacy programs and native Alaskan religious and social rituals. KBRW is a community bulletin board—its popular daily half-hour "Birthday Program" allows listeners to send greetings over the air to family and friends (apologies to Willard Scott). And "Tundra Drums" is a message service for people who lack access to telephones; listeners phone the messages in, and eight times daily Top of the World Radio spreads the word throughout its community about planes to be met and packages, mail, supplies and groceries to be picked up at the store. Such segments are a staple of rural Alaskan radio, providing the model for disc jockey Chris in the Morning on television's "Northern Exposure."

But fiction is rarely more colorful than truth—KBRW's program schedule is rounded out with call-ins on local issues, such as the complaints of native Alaskan whalers that the sound of oil drilling was driving off the whales. Music ranges from country to classical to the Grateful Dead Hour, sports from City League softball to the Iditarod dogsled race.

"We're something for everybody," says KBRW General Manager Don Rinker, an Arizona native who has also run public and commercial broadcast stations "outside" (as Alaskans refer to the lower 48 states). "The environment is harsh and hostile, but the people here are warm and friendly. They appreciate what radio can do for them."

And, at the top of the world, Alaskans know what radio does for them— friend, companion, entertainer and town crier. "Jim Johnson: Your diesel engine parts will arrive at the airfield sometime this afternoon. You can pick them up at the store."

KBBW—Two Parts Prayer, One Part Politics

During the 51-day standoff in 1993 between federal authorities and the Branch Davidian religious cult near Waco, Texas, the local Christian radio station, KBBW, sponsored prayer vigils in an attempt to bring a peaceful close to the crisis. Led by station staffers, about 50 people gathered in downtown Waco to pray that cult leader David Koresh would lead his followers out.

"There is no weapon more powerful than prayer," explained Bill Thrasher, the station's operations manager.

In many ways, KBBW typifies contemporary modern Christian radio in America—part prayer, part politics, all activist. Like other Christian broadcasters, the 10,000-watt KBBW-AM (1010) draws in equal parts upon the power of God and the electromagnetic spectrum, mobilizing listeners in support of the conservative Christian political and social agenda, local and national. When Planned Parenthood of Central Texas sought last year to establish a clinic in Waco, KBBW rallied the area's Christian community to block it; so far, the clinic has been unable to hire a fulltime physician.

At the beginning of the Clinton administration, KBBW and other Christian radio and TV stations nationwide brought the wrath of their listeners down on Congress after Clinton proposed lifting the ban on gays in the military. Christian broadcasters encouraged listeners to phone in, and more than 400,000 calls inundated Capitol Hill switchboards. The Rev. Pat Robertson, a 1988 presidential hopeful and founder of the Christian Broadcasting Network, says the "secular media" won't fight for family values, so it's up to Christian broadcasters.

There are more than 1,100 of them on the radio—about one of every 10 U.S. stations. Split roughly between the AM and FM bands, about two of three Christian stations are commercial. Some are old-style, dominated by fire-and-brimstone preachers, often seeking donations and offering organ music. Many others, like KBBW in Waco, are programmed with the staples of modern radio, but from a Christian perspective. The Waco station plays Christian rock and country music, as well as gospel and inspirational recordings. KBBW produces a local call-in show every day, carries a national talk show—CBN's syndicated "America Talks With Craig Smith"—and offers local newscasts throughout the day.

Like its secular counterparts, KBBW battles for market share. In the powerful Dallas/Fort Worth market just 90 miles away, there are 13 religious radio stations, some overlapping KBBW's coverage area. Nonetheless, KBBW's Thrasher says, "Most of our advertisers aren't looking at numbers. They want a special audience: our strong, loyal, Christian conservative audience."

Despite the political clout of that audience, however, Christian stations like KBBW are worried about the Clinton administration. An issue that looms large is the possible reinstatement of the Fairness Doctrine, dropped by the Federal Communications Commission in 1987, requiring broadcasters to report on controversial issues in their communities and to present both sides. If the Clinton adminstration reinstates the doctrine, many Christian broadcasters fear that would force them to air views with which they disagree—gay and abortion rights, for instance. If so, an arcane piece of broadcasting regulation may become the next hot topic on the Christian airwaves in Waco and elsewhere.

Viva Cuba!—Radio-Fe, Miami's "Voice of Cuban Faith"

Haunted by the death threats, Emilio Milian, then news director of Miami's WQBA-AM in Miami, bought a .357 magnum, loaded it and kept it in his car glovebox. For two years, it sat there. Then one day in 1976, on his call-in talk show, Milian charged anti-Castro terrorists were trying to assassinate opponents in Miami.

"I called them criminals," he said later. "I was, I believe, the only newsman that criticized, very hard, the terrorists." The same day, a caller threatened to kill him.

After work, Milian got into his Chevrolet station wagon, turned the key and a bomb tore off his legs. The .357 burned in the glovebox.

Now, 17 years later, Milian is unrepentant. "I have to tell what I think to the people," he says. "And I believe that I am telling the right thing. I was not afraid. I am not afraid." Today Milian runs a 50,000-watt AM station in Miami, WWFE (670), heard as far away as his Caribbean island home town of Sagua La Grande, on the island of Cuba.

He named the Spanish-language station Radio Fe, which means "faith." "It doesn't mean only that you are religious and believe in God," he says. "You can show faith in a person, or a principle, an idea." Milian's faith in a free Cuba is absolute.

On the air since 1989, Radio Fe is sort of a family business. Milian's wife, Emma Mirtha, is a secretary. His son, Emilio Jr., manages sales. Geared toward males aged 18 to 49, Radio Fe garnered 1 percent of the market in Miami's winter Arbitron ratings. The station's purpose: To be an independent voice. On-air callers can speak from any political view.

That freedom is not as automatic in Miami as it is elsewhere, at least not when the topic is Cuba. At some of the 10 other Spanish-language stations in Dade County, where 29 percent of residents are Cuban and many fled Fidel Castro's Cuba, voicing opinions considered "soft" on Castro can bring a swift hang-up, at best. Not on Radio Fe.

"With my talk show," explains Milian, who hosts "Habla El Pueblo" (The People Speak), "a communist can speak. That is something that I pride myself on."

But free speech doesn't come cheap. After the April 1976 bombing, Milian was out of the on-air business for 10 years. "I never had doubts I would reach my goal," he said after coming back.

"Of course, I cannot run. But neither can I kneel."

There were other instances of Milian's inability to kneel. After a WWFE satire called "La Mogolia" (the mess) criticized an official at the bank holding the station's $500,000 loan, the banker told Milian to cancel the show. "Go to hell," Milian responded. The bank canceled its advertising, recalled the loan and Radio Fe filed for bankruptcy in August 1991. A judge set an asking price of $2.7 million for the station, but the bank asked for less because it had found a buyer. The would-be purchasers included members of the Cuban American National Foundation, the nation's most powerful Cuban exile group, which has a history of conflict with Milian and Radio Fe (the foundation once complained to the FCC that Milian had permitted personal attacks on CANF officials.) Rather than be squelched by political rivals, Milian kept his station when a group of investors, including his son, paid $2.7 million in March 1993.

Milian presses on. For him, 17 years after the car bombing that nearly cost him his life, radio is not just culture or entertainment or happy talk, but a means of giving voice to a cause. "When you are a newsman, a journalist, and you feel that you are free—a free man, free person," he says, "you have to hold that all the way."

Closing the KAVE—Satellite's Blow to Counterculture

Candlelight vigils are not uncommon in Eugene, Oregon. University students and friends of this counterculture enclave turn out regularly to demonstrate for and against a broad menu of causes. But the several hundred people gathered in Eugene's downtown pedestrian mall on a rainy night in February 1993 were mourning an unusual victim—their beloved progressive-rock radio station.

The closing of KAVE-FM (95.3) hit Eugene's yuppies and aging hippies hard. Even the local newspaper lamented "The KAVE's" passing in an editorial. Here was a radio station that for two-and-a-half years had rebelled against the homogeneity of hit radio, whose ancestors were the free-form FM rockers of the late 1960s and '70s. The laid-back jocks on The KAVE broke the rules, venturing deep into a recording to find an obscure cut, following an Elvis Costello song with Frank Sinatra. They played blues, local artists, women's music and sponsored concerts by little-known but promising bands with names such as the Crash Test Dummies.

"You're the guys who rode into town on white horses and saved Eugene radio," a distraught listener told afternoon DJ "Bear" Corkery, just before the end. "What happened?"

What happened was the tyranny of the radio marketplace—"the end" was what some fear is the grim future of independent radio. The KAVE's owners were three thirtysomething guys from New Jersey and New York who left their jobs with law firms and advertising agencies to buy a failing Oregon college-town station and to do radio the way they knew it should be done. But The KAVE never made money. "We lost $10,000 in our best month," says co-owner Eric Alterman—and that in a small market with three other FMs playing different varieties of rock 'n' roll.

The KAVE's last set of Arbitron ratings, in fall 1992, placed the station fifth in the market with a 6.6 share—The KAVE's final riff. Station staffers argued that their listeners weren't the kind to fill out ratings books; one went so far as to write an op-ed column for the local paper attacking Arbitron's methodology. Maybe, but no matter. With one week's notice, the owners told the staff they were abandoning the progressive format in favor of "Z-Rock," a nationally syndicated, hard-rock music service. "Z-Rock" is delivered by satellite, so there's no need for disc jockeys, only salespeople. Eleven KAVE employees were laid off.

In the calculus of contemporary radio, the move makes good business sense. The KAVE's owners cut their personnel costs considerably and, with the switch of another Eugene station from rock to country, now there's elbowroom in the rock niche. But co-owner Jordan Seaman still feels "like Dr. Frankenstein. I feel like it was my job to make this thing defy the odds."

But this curious radio play didn't end there. As former KAVE staffers went hunting for investors to buy back the station and restore the progressive format, the KAVE's owners merged with the Eugene school district's failing student radio station, KRVM, turning over a 2,500 compact disc music library. In return, the student station will carry the original eclectic KAVE format from 6 a.m. to 7 p.m. and the school district will pay KAVE owners a percentage of noncommercial KRVM's listener contribution and underwriting revenues.

So is The KAVE dead, or not? For the KAVE faithful, it may not feel the same with KRVM's staff—an amalgam of green high school students and community volunteers—but at least the music is back. Still, the KAVE story may be a frightening harbinger for other independents in the tough economics of the satellite age.

"The Fan"—In the Big Apple, All-Sports, All the Time

It's sometime after 3 a.m. and Doug, a Chicago Bulls fan calling from Brooklyn, has just bet Steve Somers, the WFAN overnight guy, that his Bulls will stomp the Knicks in an anticipated NBA playoff match-up. The stakes: two pizzas (Sicilian, no anchovies). It's a typical night at New York's WFAN-AM (660)—"The Fan"—the nation's first all-sports station. All night, insomniac sports nuts from all over call in to straighten out the Yankees, to gripe about the "miserable" Mets and their manager, or to predict more greatness for Patrick Ewing and the Knicks next season. Scores, slam dunks, ERAs and RBI, armchair managing, trades, free agents and superstar wannabes—all day, every day. It's nonstop sports, sports, sports at The Fan.

Born in July 1987 as the nation's first all-sports station in what the *New York Times* termed "radio's all-sports gamble," WFAN has grown from a floundering shoestring to second in revenues ($29 million) in the country's largest media market behind all-news pioneer WINS. Emmis Broadcasting took the "gamble" when it pulled the plug in 1987 on its country music station, which was losing $500,000 a year on country music and earning $700,000 on Mets broadcasts. The owners switched call letters and format, added a 50,000-watt clear-channel frequency, landed morning schlock-talk jock Don Imus from WNBC and went into the sports business. Less than five years later, in April 1992, Infinity Broadcasting bought The Fan for a cool $70 million, then the highest selling price ever for an AM stand-alone. Warmed by that kind of success, others were prompted to try the all-sports gamble, and now at least 20 stations nationwide talk sports most or all of their programming day.

The Fan's on-air personalities are versed as much in the art of cultivating a clubby locker-room setting for its almost exclusively white, male listenership as they are in sports esoterica; New York fans, proud to be called the country's most rabid, provide the local color. In six years the station has quickly established its own niche in a wildly competitive market, emerging as a must-listen for fanatical and casual sports fans alike.

And it's not just sports fans who see the Fan as an important vehicle—WFAN makes its own news. In April 1992, then-Governor Bill Clinton, seeking to cast himself as everyman for New York's Democratic presidential primary, phoned the station and went a few well-publicized rounds with morning show host Imus. Other area politicos—U.S. Sen. Alfonse D'Amato, New Jersey Gov. Jim Florio and Connecticut Gov. Lowell Weicker—are regular Imus guests. When an alert Knicks fan found an Indiana Pacers playbook in a LaGuardia Airport waiting room, Imus made news by reading it on the air before the playoffs.

Imus aside, the station has drawn on-air talent from newspapers and network and local television while cultivating home-grown personalities tuned to the ears of the New York sports audience. New York *Daily News* columnist Mike Lupica and former CBS sports analyst Mike Francessa host daily shows. Francessa and sidekick Chris "Mad Dog" Russo, both with what must be the thickest New York accents on the air anywhere, host the station's popular afternoon drive-time show. Sounding more like bickering brothers than on-air hosts, Russo and Francessa take as much pleasure getting a rise out of each other as they do landing points against the latest target of a fickle New York sports crowd.

Despite the demise of the much promoted *National* sports daily, there is no indication that all-sports radio in general and WFAN in particular will suffer a similar fate. The *National* promised an upscale readership but wound up delivering an audience of fanatics who watched sports, read the *National* and apparently didn't do much else. But in the Big Apple, where raucous, arm-waving disputes over the relative merits of the Yanks and the Mets are as commonplace as yellow cabs, the exploits of nine New York-area professional sports teams, on and off the field, provide more than enough year-round grist for fans of the Fan, the all-sports gamble that paid off big.

Coming of Age—Pacifica Revisited

Boy, are the times a-changin' at Pacifica's KPFA in Berkeley.

Located in the mecca of American counterculture, the flagship of the Pacifica Foundation's five noncommercial stations has a rich history that left an indelible mark on public radio. Founded in 1949 by disaffected commercial radio journalist Lewis Hill, KPFA-FM (94.1) sought to promote peace, social justice, the labor movement and the arts. Indeed, the station pioneered such concepts as seeking financial support from listeners, involving community volunteers in program production and broadcasting minority viewpoints (such as those of Korean War opponents and marijuana smokers during the 1950s). Its unabashed left-wing stance brought challenges to its license renewal by the Federal Communications Commission, as well as FBI and Congressional probes into alleged communist influence.

But today, a bit longer in the tooth, this fortysomething radical is undergoing a midlife crisis. At issue is KPFA management's efforts to improve the station's "sound." The schedule has long been a meld of music shows and programs aimed at women, gays, African Americans, Asian Americans, Latinos and many others, often produced by volunteer programmers who deliver lengthy on-air monologues. A recent consultant's report cautioned, however, that the programming on KPFA and other Pacifica stations represented "castor oil" radio—"good for you but not necessarily easy to take."

"Really," station manager Pat Scott told a Bay Area weekly, "most of that stuff is unlistenable."

In response, she cancelled some of the volunteer programming in favor of a more uniform, professionally produced format of music and public affairs that includes national news programs from Pacifica's Washington production facility. Displaced volunteers were invited to audition for their old jobs. "We're getting away from equating being progressive with being unprofessional," Scott says.

Dissident volunteers and listeners revolted. The "KPFA Listeners Participation Group" has attacked the station as undemocratic and insensitive to multiculturalism. Graffiti on the wall of the station labeled Scott a "yuppie Stalinist." In addition, the Listeners Group has criticized Pacifica's plans to seek foundation funding to help pay for national programming initiatives (Pacifica will not accept money from corporate foundations, only nonprofits). The "NPR-ization" of KPFA is near, the critics warn, a reference to complaints that National Public Radio has lost its alternative edge and joined the media mainstream.

Internecine conflict is nothing new to KPFA; founder Lewis Hill himself was ousted during an episode of mid-1950s infighting. But this latest round represents KPFA's struggle to find a place, in middle age, in the changed mediascape of a changing radio world. KPFA has moved its studios from a converted cold-water flat that it had leased for four decades into a state-of-the-art $3.5-million facility, built with funds collected in a capital campaign. Now longtime Pacifica watchers wonder: Will the station continue to carry the torch for the left, or seek to become more "accessible" in the post-Cold War, Bill and Hillary era?

Radio AAHS—Kids on the Air

Used to be, one Minnesota mother says, her children woke her up scared in the middle of the night when they had bad dreams. But now, she says, the kids just turn on Radio AAHS, a rare throwback to simpler times when radio was the child's companion.

Radio AAHS is a 24-hour, satellite-delivered children's program service based in Minneapolis and carried by AM stations in 11 markets, including Los Angeles and Washington, D.C. Conventional wisdom held that kids wouldn't listen to radio. But the heck with that, says Christopher Dahl, president of Children's Broadcasting Corporation—there was nothing there for kids. Radio AAHS is an answer for kids, parents and broadcasters alike.

Dahl tested his theory that kids and radio *do* mix by purchasing a struggling Minneapolis AM station, WWTC (1280), which had already run through a variety of formats. WWTC went all-kids in 1990, adopting the name "Radio AAHS" and programming a mix of children's music, storytelling, nighttime lullabies, kid's news, call-ins and contests and "brain games" for parents to play with their children. Sure, there are some adults on the air, but Radio AAHS is kid-driven, which means the station is on the same wavelength as its young listeners. For example, one Radio AAHS senior executive is Jimmy Freeman (now 12), vice president of fun, who hosts a call-in show and answers letters from listeners about "what they think would be fun for the station to do." As Radio AAHS gradually caught on with Twin Cities listeners, advertisers slowly followed, and other cities have steadily signed up.

Fun aside, there are bills to pay. Advertisers were leery, wanting to see documented audience levels, which is difficult since ratings services measure listeners age 12 and up. But national advertisers with a history of buying kid's TV, such as McDonald's, were drawn to the station, and

Radio AAHS raised its local profile by sponsoring well-attended events like a "Kidstock" concert, featuring children's artists.

WWTC also commissioned a telephone survey to measure listening. The result, says Dahl—Radio AAHS was tops in the market for 4- to 9-year-olds. And because children often dictate what their parents listen to, there are adults in the audience, too. Radio AAHS showed up in the ratings book for men 18 to 35 on Saturday afternoons, prime time for parents to chauffeur their children around.

Once WWTC proved itself modestly successful in Minneapolis, Dahl put Radio AAHS on the satellite in 1992 and began signing up affiliates among AM stations looking for a market niche, including a trio of co-owned stations in Virginia and Maryland that now cover the Washington-Baltimore corridor with Radio AAHS.

Radio AAHS is not alone in the children's radio market. KidStar Radio, a 24-hour AM station targeting 3- to 11-year-olds, is new from Seattle, and the Children's Syndicated Radio Network broadcasts out of Michigan. Trade publications report that ABC Radio and Disney are considering a joint kid's network. Competitors? No problem, says Radio AAHS President Bill Barnett: "It would show advertisers out there that this thing works."

Grand Ole Opry—The Mother Church of Country Music

One evening in 1927, NBC's renowned music commentator Dr. Walter Damrosch rubbed a Tennessee radio announcer the wrong way and inspired perhaps the most famous ad lib in radio history. Damrosch told a nationwide audience on the "Music Appreciation Hour" that there was no place in music classics for realism. In a Nashville radio studio, George D. Hay was waiting to introduce WSM radio's "Barn Dance," a jam session of local overall-clad musicians that was about as real as it gets. After Damrosch signed off, Hay quipped: "For the past hour, we've been listening to music taken largely from Grand Opera. From now on, we will present the Grand Ole Opry."

The musicians liked the name and it stuck, today the Grand Ole Opry is the longest-running show in radio history (including its two years as the "Barn Dance"). The "Mother Church of Country Music" has featured country legends such as Patsy Cline, Roy Acuff and Hank Williams Sr. Keeping pace with the hottest format in radio in the 1990s, the

Opry's current regulars include Reba MacIntire, Garth Brooks, Randy Travis and Emmy Lou Harris. As many as two dozen stars and new artists grace the stage of the opulent Grand Ole Opry House in Nashville for each two-and-a-half-hour live broadcast, singing a song or two, telling jokes and then milling around on stage while Opry announcers read commercial spots. The show is one of Nashville's most popular tourist attractions, a tough ticket to find during the summer.

Once derided as "hick," country is now the most popular music on radio, with 2,573 stations—26.4 percent of commercial stations—in that format, far ahead of the number two format, adult contemporary, with 1,618 (16.6 percent) of U.S. radio stations. In April 1993, the National Association of Broadcasters acknowledged that fact and honored the Opry with induction into NAB's Broadcasting Hall of Fame. "The Opry has had an undeniable influence on the emergence of country music as a major force in radio," said Wayne Vriesman, chair of NAB's Radio Board.

The program's influence upon WSM-AM (650) and its corporate parent, Gaylord Entertainment, is similarly indisputable. The Opry is the linchpin of Gaylord's enterprises, which include the Opryland theme park, anchored by the Opry House, and cable's Nashville Network and Country Music Television. The popularity of the country format has led to the type of fragmentation seen in rock radio—traditional country, new country, country hits, etc. The magic of the Opry, says country star Ricky Scaggs, is that it's the one place on the radio where both old and new can be heard.

Live Friday and Saturday night broadcasts of the Grand Ole Opry are a major revenue source for all-country WSM-AM at a time when many AM music stations are struggling. The station sells 26 program sponsorships that range from $50,000 to $100,000 annually, as well as spot announcements. Some sponsors have been associated with the program for decades; for others, there's a waiting list. "They're buying not just a spot but a concept, a piece of Americana, a part of tradition," says Kyle Cantrell, a WSM personality and Opry announcer.

Al Stavitsky is assistant professor of journalism and communication at the University of Oregon in Eugene.

Sally Deneen, a free-lance writer from Fort Lauderdale, contributed the report on WWFE—Radio Fe, and Robert Westervelt, a former Media Studies Journal *editorial assistant, reported on WFAN.*

10

Music Radio—The Fickleness
of Fragmentation

Sean Ross

In a world where fragmentation explains so much—from the decline of the Big Three networks to "cookies 'n' mint" ice cream—it is tempting to view today's music-radio scene as the ultimate triumph of niche marketing. It's easy for industry pundits to assume that A (more signals) + B (more choices) = C (fewer dynasties). Were that entirely true, it would account for many stations' problems.

Fragmentation is the most-cited explanation for top-40 music radio's declining ratings and revenues, and the resulting exodus to other formats by station after station. No self-respecting listener will ever tolerate rap, rock and country together, radio programmers believe, even though that's exactly what kids at high school dances want.

Music market fragmentation is why all stations are headed for a three share, say radio executives—with the glut of new signals, they argue, no single station will ever control a market like the top-40 AMs of old did. This is why owners feel compelled to use the Federal Communications Commission's newly relaxed duopoly rules to collect two or three FMs in a market. Yet, many country stations often control 10 percent to 20 percent of their markets, and many did so long before the recent much-publicized country boom.

Does today's FM listener have choices that weren't available a decade ago? Sure. Seven years ago, the oldies format barely existed on FM and classic rock barely existed at all, but now most markets have at least one of each. You want diversity? In Los Angeles, the new No. 1

station is an 8-month-old FM specializing in "banda," a polka-like Mexican subgenre that, despite being a century old, barely existed as a commercial radio entity until the last few years.

And there *are* more FM signals than before. During the 1980s, numerous small-town stations upgraded their signals to chase larger markets they were never intended to serve. They were joined by a slew of new FMs, ostensibly intended to bolster minority ownership, though they rarely did so. Some of those new stations are still signing on, even though many existing stations are losing money.

The fragmentation theory doesn't account for everything, however. Some large markets reached their limit of available signals years ago, but the trends in New York and Washington, D.C., are about the same as in Las Vegas, which has gotten four new FMs since 1988. Besides, even markets with new FMs have lost a like number of once-viable music AMs since the 1970s, stations that once fragmented the market before going all-talk or all-ethnic. Or silent.

If music radio were truly fragmented, Miami should still have an easy listening station, Seattle should still have commercial jazz, and Detroit should still have an FM home for rhythm and blues (R&B) oldies. These are formats that make sense for their market's demographics, but they're choices that have disappeared in those towns just since 1991. If there was really a radio station for every taste these days, New York City would have a place where adult R&B fans could go without enduring the rap songs their kids like. But the Big Apple doesn't have that *or* a rap station. Then again, Las Vegas doesn't have a commercial outlet specializing in black music of any stripe, even though the nonprofit R&B station there has led the market on occasion.

There's no rule that the new FM stations have to go boldly where no other station has gone before, especially if it means serving anybody outside the prime 25-to-44 demographic that ad buyers desire most. For every broadcaster who fills an unmet need, there are three who will swarm into today's hot format, whether there's room there or not, then head off somewhere else if they don't see immediate results.

This boom-bust cycle is such a constant in radio that if you look at the last 14 years alone, you can already see it repeating itself in more than one format. Disco boomed in 1978, died by 1980 and revived in 1986. Alternative rock stations went through one millisecond's boom in 1983 after the rise of MTV; now they're back.

Jazz virtually disappeared from the commercial FM band during the 1980s; so did Jackson Browne/Joni Mitchell "mellow rock." By the early 1990s, both formats had been reborn and reissued as "new AC" (adult contemporary) and "rock AC," respectively. But these born-again formats are already losing stations because their payoff hasn't been large or fast enough for fickle or financially strapped operators.

Hard-rock radio stations are back, even though they—and the album-rock format in general—were pronounced dead in 1983. Country had the same problem a few years later, when many of the stations that had swarmed into the format during the "Urban Cowboy" boom rode off into some sunset somewhere. So perhaps today's top-40 programmer can take some comfort in knowing that the format's recent travails aren't so different from country music's mid-'80s woes. Looking at the boom in new country FMs, one can only hope that top 40 "dies" as successfully as country did.

Certainly, top 40 has little other reason for optimism at the moment. The format is losing several prominent stations a month, including some that survived the early '80s unscathed. When those stations change, their old listeners don't go to the remaining top-40 station in the market, assuming there is one—they scatter to other formats or to MTV or to their tape decks.

Of the stations that still consider themselves top 40, few fit the old definition of playing all the hits, regardless of genre. Many are closer to adult contemporary stations or album rockers or even alternative stations. Many are, essentially, R&B stations that hope they can avoid the advertiser bias that plagues the format by insisting that they're something else. Those station managers would deny that this is their motivation, of course, at least publicly—theirs are the new top-40 stations of the 1990s. But it's more accurate to say that they're what listeners are choosing in top 40's absence. Top 40 is, by definition, a broad-based format. It has withered. It could even die. But it cannot be redefined—top 40 that sounds like urban or adult contemporary (AC) or album-oriented rock (AOR) is not top 40.

Even broad-based top 40s have done plenty of swarming. Since 1987, they have been through the Madonna-led dance revival, the Guns 'n' Roses "headband" era, the rise of rap and hip-hop, the rap backlash and now a fascination with alternative rock. All of this darting from one craze to another gave one segment after another of top 40's one-time coalition audience the signal to get lost. Men were chased away by the emphasis on dance music. Then women left during the hard-rock era. Now teens are being shooed away.

Through all this purging of current listeners, old top-40 listeners rarely came back. Many stations have backed away from rap and R&B and emphasized 1980s oldies in an attempt to reclaim their adults. Judging from the ratings, older listeners aren't getting that message, but teens are. In 1989, top 40 controlled about 60 percent of the teen audience; now it's about 40 percent of those who actually still listen to radio, not counting the teen-agers who've abandoned it for MTV, Nintendo or their Walkmen.

Beyond the general crisis of confidence, top 40 also lacks a particular kind of sound—the medium-weight, up-tempo pop-rock hit that moms and kids can agree on. In the mid-1980s, songs like Michael Jackson's "Beat It" or Van Halen's "Jump" defined the format. Now that kind of record shows up every few months at best, just often enough to prove that somebody misses it. Even urban radio, which remains relatively healthy, lacks up-tempo sound to balance rap and R&B ballads.

That is where country radio has made its mark. After years of providing a relatively sedate product, Nashville now sounds a lot like a new Motown, rolling out a steady supply of up-tempo records, some of them great, many of them just great-sounding. These hits are smooth enough for older listeners who don't like rap; they're hot enough for kids who felt betrayed when top 40 backed away from rap and dance and couldn't offer anything worth listening to as a replacement. Country music's teen market share has exploded and there is only the thinnest evidence that encouraging teens will turn off the older, more entrenched core audience.

But we know from years of boom-bust activity what will happen next, even if it takes a while. Both Sacramento and Pittsburgh—neither particularly obvious as country markets—now have three country FMs each. Just since January, Syracuse has gone from one country FM to four. So far, adding a second country station in a market has tended to expand the country audience (but that doesn't guarantee that Syracuse will support four country stations any more than Milwaukee did four top 40s in 1984—all four Milwaukee top 40s are gone now).

New FCC ownership rules mean that a top-40 or adult-contemporary station can buy a second FM and go country in an attempt to erode the

MUSIC RADIO FORMATS

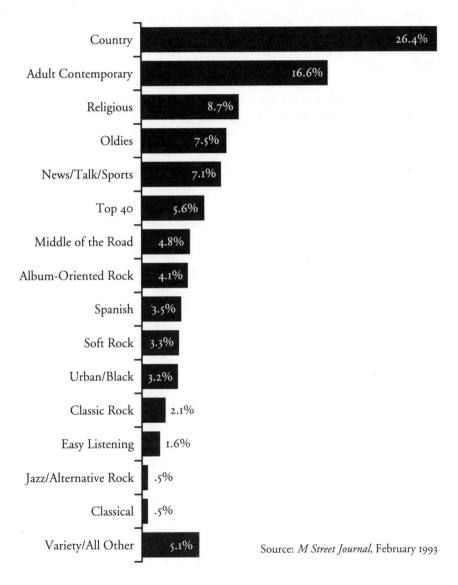

Source: *M Street Journal,* February 1993

shares of the existing country competitor. Or that the existing country station can open a second in an attempt (usually unsuccessful) to create its own competition before somebody else does. Country radio is a natural place for swarming these days, and the new ownership rules will only make it worse.

Will country radio fragment into different subformats? It hasn't yet, despite years of predictions to the contrary. Many stations call themselves "hot country" or "young country"; some offer a few more oldies than others; but most are playing the same music regardless of how they package it. The rare attempts at progressive country or country-rock usually end up sounding homogenized. Therein lies another truth about music radio that explains as much as fragmentation. Not only are more stations competing for fewer dollars, but they're competing for them only in formats that target 25- to 44-year-olds because radio can't seem to sell anything else.

With all that in mind, having already addressed country, let's look at the prognosis for the other major radio formats.

Adult contemporary: If there's any format that *does* display the ravages of fragmentation, it's AC. There used to be just one pop format that fit in between rock 'n' roll and easy listening, softer than top 40 and brighter than easy listening. Now there are at least three—soft, mainstream and "hot" adult contemporary. And those listeners are being stolen by country and oldies stations as well. AC still controls a lot of listening, but it depends on top 40 to find records that will eventually become familiar enough for older audiences. If top 40 doesn't rebound, AC's music supply could dry up.

Oldies: Most sizable markets have an oldies FM station now. But few cities have demonstrated the ability to support two, which means that the format's growth will either be in smaller markets or where the first station is weak. Most oldies stations are centered on top-40 gold from the years 1964 to 1971, meaning that no one under age 30 grew up with their music. For a while, younger listeners were coming to oldies radio just for something different, but now they've discovered country, leaving oldies radio with a finite audience. The next logical step would seem to be a 1970s oldies format. A few smaller stations have tried it, but there are few owners brave enough to offer a steady diet of "Little Willy" and "You Sexy Thing." Yet.

Urban contemporary: Ratings look pretty good for R&B radio, and if you add in the stations that are really urban but won't admit it, they look even better. In markets where top 40 is disappearing, the kids need somewhere else to go and urban is already the No. 2 teen format. This despite the fact that many urban FMs serve the younger audience only reluctantly. Most have been holding the line on rap to keep urban AC stations from stealing their adults. This strategy doesn't always work, but it's been surprisingly sturdy in a lot of markets.

Alternative rock: This, along with country, is the boom format of the moment. In 1983, Cleveland and Bakersfield were getting "modern rock" stations (regardless of whether they wanted them). Now the format is popping up across the heartland again. The problem is that alternative stations draw a small but vocal core which resents any attempts to invite in other listeners. In San Francisco or Boston, there might be enough ad dollars for modern rock to operate as a boutique, but one wonders if you could say the same thing in Lincoln, Neb.

Album rock: When classic rock hit in the mid-'80s, most album rock outlets tried to kill the new format by coopting it and playing a ton of older rock themselves. Now, a slew of younger, edgier groups have come along and many wonder if 20- and 40-year-olds can be satisfied with the same rock. That's why there are hard-rock FMs popping up again with slogans like "less music by dead guys." But there are still plenty of old-rock FMs playing only two current songs an hour.

Classic rock: This is the only one of today's major formats that didn't exist until the mid-'80s. When it was new and novel, classic rock could come to town and draw a bigger crowd than the regular AOR station. Eventually, it settled into a smaller, but very comfortable niche. The biggest exceptions are in New York and Philadelphia, where the success of Howard Stern has allowed classic rockers to all but dismantle the competition. Now Stern is syndicated and one station has even become the market's second classic rocker just to be his affiliate. This is why we should discuss a format unexpected in this context: Talk.

Talk: Stern isn't the only high-profile rock 'n' talk personality being syndicated. So many morning shows have gone national in recent months that many stations, especially rock outlets, have gone to talk during other parts of the day to accommodate them. Eventually, pundits say, some rock FMs will segue to talk once their audience finally tires of hearing "Black Dog" for the 8,000th time. Music radio has streamlined its presentation to the point where most jocks outside morning drive do very little but introduce songs, which creates a great opportunity for younger-demographic talk radio. Amy Fisher, "the Long Island Lolita," going on the air with Stern is the 1990s version of New York's top-40 power-house WABC helping Ringo Starr find his St. Christopher medal in 1964. Small-town DJs who used to rush out to their cars at night to hear WABC or the other 50,000-watt AM rockers now sneak out at lunch to hear Rush Limbaugh. And that highlights the need for music radio in any format to create its own excitement and leads us back to...

Top 40: In 1981, the station credited with rejuvenating the format, Philadelphia's WCAU-FM, was a screaming top-40 outlet that repeated its hits once an hour and played three or four jingles between records. If WCAU was obnoxious, it was also an instant success and the music it played was secondary to the attention it commanded. Top 40 could do that again. In fact, with the adults too busy to spend much time with the radio and the kids too distracted by TV and video games, showmanship improves the chances of drawing a crowd. Some top-40 stations sound better these days. Several have taken their lead from New York's once-mighty Z100, which, realizing that adults aren't buying into a more adult format, has finally come to grips with sounding younger and hipper. Top 40's prospects may also depend on Bill Clinton. When the national mood improved for a while in the early Reagan years, top 40 rebounded. Call them polar opposites, but country and urban both help their audiences make sense out of a distressing world. Those needs could change if the national outlook brightens.

Radio has always been the most cyclical of media, a medium where those who cannot remember the past are doomed to repeat it, recycling oldies every 28 hours or so. Even in its current state, it's not so daring to predict an eventual top-40 comeback; it's the only format with nowhere left to go but up. What might break the cycle are more changes in the physical landscape, and there are some signs of those changes:

1. Because the FCC now allows owners to have more than one FM in a market, some broadcasters could decide that not every property has to be a mass-appeal format with boxcar numbers. That could lead broadcasters to conclude that top 40 is worth doing, even if its numbers never rebound, or that some of the more eclectic choices are worth offering. We haven't seen much of this so far, but the rules are new.

2. For the first time in 40 years, we are seeing a rise in national radio. Stern and Limbaugh are already stars. Satellite networks, which cover about 20 percent of America's stations with their programming, are proliferating and starting to emphasize more big-name talent. There are already satellite networks in several niche formats and they have the

economies of scale to offer other formats that might not be profitable for a single operator.

3. If none of this forces operators to diversify, the end of commercial radio as we know it may take place when digital audio broadcasting (DAB) becomes a reality. Local owners' worst nightmare is a handful of satellite superstations making local radio obsolete; those stations, too, could offer many things a local operator could not.

Already, the diversity that people think accompanied music radio's fragmentation is offered by a number of national multichannel digital services fed through local cable operators—a sneak preview of one future for music radio. Offerings have ranged from British rebroadcasts to progressive country and most points in between—in short, the kind of program diversity that should accompany fragmentation, but hasn't. So far these services are well-kept secrets; they cost money and you can't carry your cable radio box to the beach with you. But nothing says they'll stay that way forever.

And how do existing stations respond to all this? At first, broadcasters hoped for government intervention. When the spectre of DAB rose in the late 1980s, the broadcast lobby scrambled to push for some sort of preemptive protections against digital megastations (which the FCC shows no inclination to provide). In fact, the FCC has suggested local broadcasters view DAB as a challenge.

Actually, that's good advice. As with most broadcast issues, the DAB question appears to be losing its urgency, not because the threat is less but because radio folk have a short attention span—the same characteristic that perpetuates the format boom-bust cycle. If the fate of top 40 bespeaks a disturbing willingness to flounder rather than fight back, so does music radio's generally turgid response to change.

Though spurned by the FCC on this issue, broadcasters still may have five good years to lobby their audiences on the value of radio as we now know it. Those boarding the national radio bandwagon must demonstrate that it offers more quality bang for the buck, not just economies of scale. Advocates of local control should renew their vows and plan a second honeymoon with their audiences, to remind them why they got together in the first place.

Sean Ross, associate editor of M Street Journal, *a radio industry newsletter, and an executive at Profile Records in New York, is former radio editor of* Billboard.

11

Whither (Or Wither?) AM?

Michael C. Keith

Is AM radio on the verge of extinction? Some in the industry—not only FM operators—believe so. Over the last two decades, listeners have steadily abandoned AM; just 20 years ago, AM comfortably claimed the bulk of the total radio listening audience, but by the late 1980s, FM had three-quarters of the audience. And in January 1992, for the first time since the medium's golden age in the 1920s, the number of AM station authorizations dropped. True, the number slipped by just three, but it's symptomatic of the medium's deepening malaise.

"We all labor against our own cure," observed 17th-century British writer Sir Thomas Browne, voicing wisdom that may bear special relevance to the predicament confronting AM radio, the eldest electronic medium. One can't help but wonder whether AM's woes are self-inflicted, and if there is any way to restore health to the ailing band. Is AM dying because it *has* static or because it *is* static?

Beginning in the late 1960s, AM's listenership declined as FM fine-tuned its sound. AM signals have wider geographic reach, but FM stereo sound is better. In 1977, AM still had over half of the radio audience, but listeners "voted with their ears," as one media historian put it, and migrated to FM. Although Arbitron figures show that in large metropolitan areas, big AM killer-signal stations, "50-kilowatt clears," often appear at or near the top of the ratings, AM claims barely 15 percent of the audience in many markets.

Trade magazines and industry conferences typically blame their AM troubles solely on FM's superior audio signal, but there are other factors as well. Almost half of AM station managers responding to a survey published in the 1993 *Journal of Radio Studies*, in fact, cited technical problems as the foremost reason for the medium's pitiable state; fewer than one-third of AM managers pointed to programming.

Poor fidelity, static, inadequate fine-tuning, programming difficulties and other factors all contribute to the withering of AM, and more investigation clearly is needed to pinpoint possible solutions. But radio, taken for granted by the public, has never been viewed as particularly worthy of scholarly attention either. There is little in academic journals on the topic of AM issues; indeed, a bibliography in the 1992 debut issue of the *Journal of Radio Studies*—the only such publication in existence—includes only one study on AM.

Technical parity with FM obviously tops the list of AM's problems. In recent years, research and development have gone into creating an improved AM receiver that features enhanced reception. New FCC certification standards for these super sets include improved frequency response—better reproduction of audio signals—noise reduction to eliminate static and extended AM broadcast band (from 1605 to 1705 KHz). The goal, of course, is to encourage manufacture of better AM receivers, which station operators hope will bring music back to the AM band. The implication is that music is a programming ingredient that AM operators see as a cure-all.

Meanwhile, the dream of AM stereo remains more a concept than a reality, even though Congress recently approved legislation forcing the FCC to select an AM stereo standard, and the Commission proposes giving exclusivity to Motorola's C-QUAM system. Many broadcasters believe this may resuscitate interest in stereo signaling among AM operators, which has waned over the years because of federal foot-dragging.

"If the FCC during Mark Fowler's era had established an advisory committee on AM stereo and then selected the system that this advisory unit recommended, there would be a lot more successful AM stations today," observes broadcaster and industry consultant Ward L. Quaal, voicing the frustration of many throughout the industry.

But even if the long-awaited AM stereo dream does materialize at last, there's little indication that anyone will care. *Audio* magazine's equipment directory is one indifference indicator—only three of 80 stereo radio tuners listed in the latest issue were for what the National Association of Broadcasters (NAB) calls AMAX (maximum AM) sets. And specifications and receiver standards for the AM equipment weren't even published. At a recent Consumer Electronics Show in Las Vegas, consumer audio companies also demonstrated apathy toward improved super set AM radios, few of which could be found on the exhibit floor. The prevailing attitude among manufacturer reps was, "Who cares?"

Signal interference remains a formidable obstacle to better AM reception. From the FCC's perspective, there are simply too many stations cluttering the band, so the Commission asked stations that create the most interference to move to the extended spectrum between 1605 and 1705 KHz. The extension offers 10 channels, which will accommodate up to 250 stations, and the FCC has imposed strict interference rules and spacing standards to ensure improved reception for stations that relocate there. The Commission statement characterizes the extension as "paving the way for better sound with a new block of high-fidelity stations and improved sound on the conventional band."

But this strategy has not been without its detractors, who have filed more than 19 petitions for reconsideration. Skeptics perceive it as entirely inadequate—a Band-Aid on a hemorrhage—and contend that a better solution to AM interstation interference would be to change existing AM signal protection ratios and methodology. For one thing, this would involve increasing the power of certain regional stations to reduce interference caused by nonbroadcast sources.

Up until the early 1990s, continuous dial tuning, featuring a contiguous AM and FM band, was considered a key ingredient to AM's resuscitation. Forcing listeners to switch from one band to another trapped AM on one side of an impenetrable wall, blocked from lucrative younger audiences who didn't know anything about AM's existence. The advent of digital touch tuning has largely eliminated these fears, although the physical barrier between AM and FM is likely to remain for many years. Regardless of the availability of either continuous dial tuning or digital touch tuning, most existing radio receivers feature two-band rotary tuning, and it will be well into the next millennium before the new tuning options percolate through the market. Furthermore, the AM-FM barrier still exists in many new digital dial tuners because the user must still manually switch from one band to the other.

Many see digital audio broadcasting (DAB) as another possible panacea, but the optimists neglect the fact that the improved in-band DAB signal for AM may be matched by even greater sound improvements in competing FM. Media researchers Arlen Diamond and James Sneegas

COMMERCIAL RADIO STATION GROWTH, 1960–1992

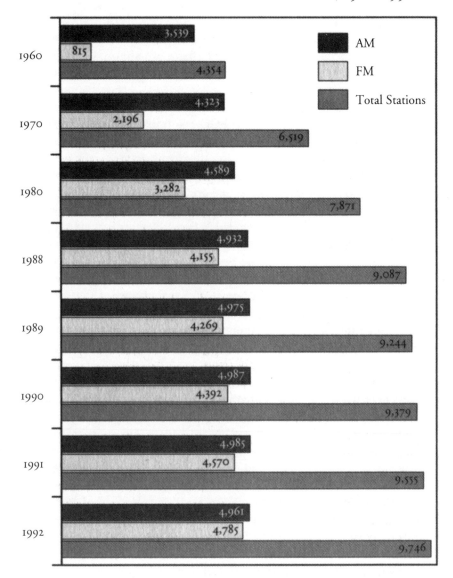

Source: *Radio & Records* Sales/Management Survey 1991;
Radio Advertising Bureau, *Radio Marketing Guide &
Fact Book,* 1993; Federal Communications Commission.

of Southwest Missouri State University suggest that while AM's reception may improve, FM signals will improve more. Because of the immutable physics of the standard broadcast band, AM will never provide as clear a signal as FM—at best, digital with static, say the skeptics.

But DAB supporters disagree, arguing that digitization will eliminate most annoyances because the signal will be processed differently and therefore be immune to atmospheric interference. Improved conversion techniques, coupled with industry and regulatory emphasis will give AM virtual parity with FM, they contend.

In recent years more and more AM-FM combo operations have resorted to simulcasting as a way to reduce expenses generated by their unprofitable AMs, another sad irony given that simulcasting originally deterred the growth of FM until the FCC limited the practice in the 1960s in markets with 100,000 listeners or more. Forcing broadcasters to originate programming on their FMs was an important step in the medium's rise to equality with AM. Today, simulcasting keeps many ailing AMs from going dark, but this may only be forestalling the inevitable.

Another hurdle may be more psychological or social than technical. For many young listeners, AM carries a stigma based on assumptions of poor signal quality and "oldie" programming aimed at the Geritol crowd. Often, AM is dismissed without a hearing. For example, researchers Diamond and Sneegas found in a 1991 study published in the *Journal of Applied Sciences* that listeners invariably assumed that inferior radio signals played in an experimental setting were AM. They weren't. A 1988 Arbitron study conducted in conjunction with the Annenberg School for Communication at the University of Pennsylvania concluded that listeners think programming is the fundamental difference between AM and FM. The belief that AM stations don't air music is responsible for the medium's loss of listeners under 35, the study concluded.

Finally, in addition to these attitudinal and technical barriers confronting AM, many AM broadcasters must cope with decaying facilities and the lack of funding for desperately needed improvements. Rotting copper radials, rusting antennas, tired transmitters and worn-out studio equipment are commonplace, and the depressed market for AM airtime only promises further erosion.

Some think concern over saving AM radio may be more emotional than practical. "How about *not* resurrecting AM?" asks communications scholar Lee Thayer. "There may be more to be gained from letting it go. Maybe energy would be better invested in seeking an entirely 'new' radio. Might not that be easier, a more modern way of approaching the issue?"

Maybe AM isn't worth saving. Even the NAB and top radio executives say there are too many stations, that over the years the FCC has been extravagant, if not profligate, in issuing construction permits. In the 1980s and early '90s alone, some 600 new radio stations were approved, to say nothing of the new intermediate classes the FCC created. Obviously, what this means is more stations vying for listeners and advertising dollars.

Internal competition is fierce throughout broadcasting, of course, and adding to radio-operator angst in the 1990s is the introduction of cable audio services, such as Digital Cable Radio and Digital Planet and the seemingly inevitable advent of direct-to-listener satellite radio formats.

In the broadcasting marketplace, as in other jungles, it comes down to the survival of the fittest. AM radio is not exactly a finely tuned athlete, either in technological or programming terms, so its slow fade to date may simply be a manifestation of Darwinism at work. On the other hand, there is a chance that reports of AM's imminent death have been greatly exaggerated. AM radio has given much to society and culture. At its best, it has been captivating, even inspiring. Some of the greatest artists of this century—Aldous Huxley, Arturo Toscanini, Marian Anderson, John Barrymore and T.S. Eliot—have graced its microphones and trekked through its precious ether, a priceless legacy. But if AM can't overcome the many troubles that have beset it, the end of the century that gave us radio could also bring its final sign-off.

Michael C. Keith, a professor of communication at Boston College and chair of education at the Museum of Broadcast Communications in Chicago, is the author of several books on broadcasting.

III

The Global Airwaves

12

Radio Beyond the Anglo-American World

Claude-Jean Bertrand

Despite some misconceptions to the contrary, most of the world's radios do not belong to British or U.S. citizens. Britons and Americans may own one-third of the estimated 2 billion radio sets in use on the planet, but 95 percent of radio listeners live outside of England and the United States. And only a tiny minority of those listeners is reached by the Voice of America, the BBC, CIA stations in Munich and U.S. short-wave religious stations. The BBC is proud of its worldwide listenership of 137 million, but that's just 2 percent of mankind.

And yet one sometimes gets the feeling that Anglo-Americans believe that their radio, like all their media, is the best in the world, that it should serve as a model, and that they themselves have nothing to learn elsewhere.

Broadcasting chronologies in U.S. textbooks make interesting reading for a European: One of them lists 68 major events in broadcasting since 1639, only nine of which are non-American. Beyond a couple of unavoidable figures such as Hertz and Marconi (but not Branly, Nipkow or Popov), you would think nothing ever happened in the realm of electronic media that was not American or, secondarily, British.

Yet much has taken place outside the United States and Great Britain that was original or influential—not just, for instance, the invention of the tape recorder (Danish and German), the videocassette player (Japanese) or the compact disk (Dutch). Admittedly, what is original is not necessarily good or better, but it deserves to be recognized.

Such is the case of wired radio. In the mid-1980s, broadcasting scholar Sidney W. Head estimated that 13 percent of the world's radio receivers were wired. In 1992, the BBC estimated the number of wired sets in Western Europe at 800,000, and 100 million in Eastern Europe. The Soviet Union at the turn of the 1980s still had more wired receivers than wireless sets. There were three main reasons for this. One was economic: Wired radio is cheaper. Another was political: Wired radio helped the Party exercise its ideological monopoly. The third was strategic: No enemy could jam wired radio (or use transmitters as homing beacons for its missiles), and it could give immediate warning in case of attack by the West. So the sets were never to be switched off. Similarly, during the Gulf War, Israeli public radio devoted one of its channels to silence overnight, so that people could sleep with their sets switched on and be sure they would be awakened in case of a Scud missile attack.

This calls to mind another originality in the former Soviet Union: the use of radio to *prevent* listening to radio by jamming foreign broadcasts over every city of 100,000 inhabitants or more. Some estimate that the Soviets spent as much on jamming as they did on broadcasting. Yet they failed to prevent their own people from listening to foreign broadcasts, just as they couldn't force other peoples to listen to the 2,000 hours of programming they beamed abroad weekly.

In the days of China's Cultural Revolution, wired radio was omnipresent, with loudspeakers (120 million of them by the late 1980s) in schools, playgrounds, factories, trains, crossroads, even fields. For Mao, radio was "the most important tool to establish the dictatorship of the proletariat," television being too expensive and print being reserved for the Mandarin caste. On the positive side, wired radio made local programming possible, in local dialects. And collective listening monitored by party members ensured that some feedback went up the bureaucratic chain of command.

Group listening was also organized in several African countries in the 1960s, for educational purposes. Starting in 1965, local teachers in Niger, equipped with tape recorders, would investigate issues in the bush and send in suggestions for programs dealing with farming or public health. Radio clubs in the villages would then listen to the programs and discuss them. The same was done in Benin.

In Africa, it was only when sets became portable and inexpensive, hence more common, that radio began to play a major role in political life. In the industrialized part of the globe, radio's impact was felt long before, especially during wars. It is worth recalling that after Japan had been hit by two A-bombs, the emperor obtained a quick end to the blood-shed through the unprecedented step of addressing his people on radio.

In Europe quite recently, in February 1981, when a few fascists from the Guardia Civil tried a coup by seizing the Spanish parliament, the team from Cadena SER, the main private radio network, fled but left their microphones switched on. Thus the whole population followed the event play by play and could mobilize for democracy. Ten years later in Russia, Radio M/Echo, a station started by the Moscow municipality and the democratic review *Ogonyok*, rallied the population against the attempted coup by Communist stalwarts, in spite of pursuit by the KGB.

The French have a long experience of history-making by radio. Everyone in France today has heard about (though few actually heard) Gen. de Gaulle's call to resistance sent June 18, 1940, on the airwaves of the BBC. And every person over the age of 60 remembers the instructions and encouragement broadcast from London by the Free French during World War II. Some 20 years later, at the end of the Algerian war, when some French army officers and colonists attempted a coup in 1961, the same de Gaulle, who had then been elected president, crushed it by radio from Paris: He ordered the rank and file, most of whom owned transistor sets, to mutiny against the leaders of the putsch.

The French are accustomed to radio from abroad. Actually, one of the most original forms of broadcasting they developed were commercial stations that addressed a French audience from transmitters abroad, located on the periphery of the country so as to escape both the state monopoly on broadcasting and the post-1945 ban on advertising.

One of those stations, Radio Luxembourg (RTL), dates back to 1933; the others appeared during or after World War II. There were four in all. Two—Radio Andorra (1940) in the Southwest and Radio Monte Carlo (1943) in the Southeast—were located in tiny principalities and were to remain regional. The other two, with transmitters abroad but studios in Paris, gradually became national: RTL with its 2,000-kw AM-LW transmitter in Luxembourg, and Europe 1 (1955), with an equally powerful transmitter in the German state of Saar. For several decades, they were the most popular radios. Listeners enjoyed their entertaining programs and political freedom; advertisers loved them at a time when public television carried no commercials.

In fact, the French state refused to relinquish its control on the airwaves, so it bought large shares in three of the largest "peripheral" stations and, to manage that stock, set up the *Société financière de radiodiffusion* (SOFIRAD). In Europe, it does not seem outrageous that a state should be part-owner of a commercial broadcaster: The Spanish state, for instance, owns 25 percent of the No. 1 radio network Cadena SER.

After the French state gave up its monopoly on radio in 1981 and on the whole of broadcasting in 1984, the stations stopped pretending they were peripheral; RTL and Europe 1 now use scores of local FM channels all over France. And they remain the most popular generalist national radios, part of an exceptionally rich radio mix that includes Radio-France's five national programs, about a dozen specialized commercial networks and hundreds of unaffiliated local stations. As for the SOFIRAD, beginning in 1986 it started selling its shares in the peripherals; the last one, Radio Monte Carlo (RMC) was privatized at the end of 1993.

The phenomenon of peripherals is not unique to France. To some extent, Deutschlandfunk, the German federal station aimed at Eastern Europe, was a peripheral station for the German Democratic Republic, and it played a major part in maintaining German unity during the years of Soviet rule. In Slovenia (the former Yugoslavia), the station Capodistria serves northern Italy, as does RMC's Italian program, while from the Vatican enclave come FM broadcasts for the citizens of Rome. And "peripherals" also exist in other parts of the world: Radio SR, for instance, which addresses South Africans from Swaziland, and the "border blaster" XERF, based in Mexico but aimed at the United States and using five times the maximum power authorized by the Federal Communications Commission.

Today, with the collapse of the Soviet Union, the 40-year radio war waged by the two superpowers has also come to an end. And only a few nations here and there—such as Iraq, Iran or North Korea—still bray the old-fashioned propaganda. But radio also can be used in the fight to achieve social change.

The United States has never experienced the phenomenon of hundreds of unauthorized radio stations, whether shipboard "pirates" or land-based "free radios," nonprofit or commercial, some adopting the professional top-40 format, others creative and amateurish (like the early Pacifica stations in the United States). All by their very existence question the status quo. Interestingly, in October 1993, after the Israeli-PLO agreement, Kol A Shalom stopped broadcasting from its boat outside Israeli territorial waters. Started in the 1960s by Abie Nathan, it broadcast pop music and peace messages in Hebrew, English, French and Arabic.

It was such unauthorized stations that, from the mid-1970s, gradually destroyed state monopolies on broadcasting across Europe, first in Italy, then in France, the Netherlands, Ireland and Greece. Being inexpensive and easy to hide or move around, radio hardware was beautifully adapted to guerrilla tactics. And such enterprises made it clear to politicians, rightwing and leftwing alike, that people wanted local radio and diverse formats. Some rulers were hard of hearing, especially in the former Soviet Union. I remember a brief item in a French daily of 1974 about some *radioizdat*, the radio version of the *samizdat*, or underground writings. Several hundred "gangsters of the airwaves" had been arrested in Donetsk because the pop music and chatter they broadcast disrupted normal industrial and commercial communications. It took the implicit message a dozen more years to get through.

Contrary to what some Americans might believe, there is not only more radio, but probably more interesting radio outside the United States than inside. One bizarre example: Galei Tsahal, the radio station of the Israeli armed forces, draws about a quarter of the Israeli audience. Why? Because it is run by energetic imaginative draftees who know what music young people like and who, being in a position to know what news is truly sensitive, don't overindulge in self-censorship.

Of course, the globe cannot be surveyed here, so I shall list just a few interesting creations, stressing the sector I know best.

Since sets became inexpensive and powered by small batteries, radio has been *the* dominant medium in underdeveloped regions, which usually have oral cultures and low literacy rates, and contain by far the majority of mankind. In the poorer parts of the planet, only the state has had the means and the motivation to set up stations. Unfortunately, while rulers talked a lot about using radio to develop their nation's economy and to promote national unity and culture, most have used radio primarily as a tool to preserve their dictatorships.

In black Africa, even now, print media are produced for an elite and television is only for city people, as are shortwave sets. Not only can few rural people afford shortwave receivers, most would not understand broadcasts in any language but their own tribal language. So they tune in to national radio; rulers can find no better tool for manipulating the masses. But for those who do own a shortwave receiver, the necessary tuning several times a day has led them to hear a variety of stations over the dial, most of them foreign. So more and more of them have access to news sent from abroad about their country, its neighbors and the rest of the world. Germany, Belgium, the Netherlands, Canada, the Vatican, China, France and others broadcast to Africa in French, English and the major native languages.

Radio also makes it possible for minority groups in poor countries to have their own media and preserve their culture, like Indian tribes in Latin America. Even in a large, fast-developing nation like Mexico, radio flourished in the 1980s, demonstrating its power during the 1985 earthquake and its independence during the 1988 elections (as opposed to television). It now shows remarkable diversity. On the one hand are the commercial stations of the media giant Televisa: 10 networks based in Mexico City serving 240 affiliates. On the other hand are the state-controlled IMER educational radio, provincial public radios in 24 of the states, 15 university radio stations and community radio in 11 languages. And finally, in the technological vanguard, there are several pay networks of digital radio distributed by multichannel multipoint distribution system (MMDS).

In no rich nation is radio dead or dying. And its variety is striking. In most parts of the world outside the United States, radio is not merely a provider of rock 'n' roll or country music, heavily larded with commercials. Americans have become accustomed to ad-laced music radio, just as they are accustomed to obesity, a mind-boggling murder rate and to doctors who don't make house calls. But just because one can get used to something does not mean it is better. The state-owned radio monopoly common to most nations from the early 1920s to the 1970s and '80s is often derided in the United States, but it established the concept of public service radio. And that tradition is probably what most makes non-U.S. radio different.

Public service means that radio is provided universally, at national, regional and local levels, whatever the density of the population; the reason the Italian constitutional court gave for breaking the RAI monopoly in 1975 was that it did not provide local service.

Public service radio serves minorities, ethnic and otherwise, even if those populations are small and poor, like the Lapps in the north of Sweden. The Special Broadcasting Service (SBS) in Australia was launched in 1975 as an experiment to serve non-WASP minorities in Sydney and Melbourne, but it grew into a state-funded institution separate from the Australia Broadcasting Corporation (ABC), the BBC-like public service monolith. SBS radio broadcasts 18 hours a day in more than 50 languages, from Arabic to Vietnamese.

Public service also means that radio is more of a parent and less of a whore; that it gives people not just what they want, but also what they need; that it promotes education and culture. NHK, the Japanese public broadcasting system, must by law operate two radio stations in every prefecture; one of its networks functions 18 hours a day and is 78 percent educational. Australia's ABC finances symphony orchestras. Public-service radio is supposed to promote national music, serious and pop, and original drama. Most of the music Radio-France puts on the air is in French, and Radio-France Internationale is expected to promote all forms of French culture abroad.

All public service radio is not funded in the same way. In France, its only resources come from a user's fee; the same for the Swedish Sveriges Radio and NHK in Japan. In Greece, funding comes from a tax added to everyone's electric bill. Some systems get all their revenue from advertising, as in Spanish public radio (RTE), and some combine fees and ads, such as Dutch radio or the Italian RAI.

And public radio is not controlled similarly everywhere. In Italy in 1975, the national networks were divided between the major blocs in parliament, RAI Uno going to the Socialists and RAI Due to the Christian Democrats. In Germany, nearly every *land*, or region, owns a radio station; while those 11 stations have formed an association, each remains independent and is governed by a board on which churches, unions and other social or cultural organizations are represented, as well as the major political parties. In Sweden, all the stock of Sveriges Radio is in the hands of representative social groups.

Perhaps the most original broadcasting structure in the world is found in the Netherlands. For many years, Dutch society was divided ideologically among the Liberal Protestants, Evangelical Protestants, Catholics and Socialists, the four "pillars." Originally, any association related to any of the "pillars" (and, since 1969, any group with at least 60,000 members) has been entitled to some airtime on the five public radio channels, on a trial basis. To make that access permanent, an association must attract at least 150,000 members, which it does mainly by publishing a TV program magazine. Groups with 300,000 subscribers are entitled to three times as much airtime; those with 450,000 get five times as much. A public institution provides coordination and produces general interest programming.

Finally, let me consider a few interesting developments in France, where one finds a few strange little fishes and two huge transnational octopuses.

As early as the 1930s and '40s, hundreds of small stations existed in Spain, parish stations that have since disappeared; today there is a general movement in Europe to expand radio to the regional and local level. Since 1978, for example, Sweden has permitted "narradios" (neighborhood radios), whose licensees rent a small transmitter from the state telecom authority. In 1992, 2,000 nonprofit associations of all kinds— local churches, unions, sports clubs, political parties, etc.—shared 160 transmitters. Norway has about the same system.

In France some of the "free" stations of the late 1970s later went commercial and have turned into mere relays for music nets; others disappeared. But the 530 or so nonprofit stations, modestly subsidized by the state ($30,000 a year on average), that remain constitute almost one-fifth of the total stations in France, just as in Italy. They have little money but rely on creativity, volunteers and public participation. They either serve a community (like the 16-year-old Radio Dreyeckland in Alsace) or a minority within a large city (like Radio-Beur in Paris for second-generation North Africans). They give the community a voice, keep its culture alive, support its initiatives. Since 1993, they have been able to subscribe to Canal A, a news-*cum*-public affairs and music network created to help "associative stations."

In the United States, the 30-odd all-news stations are essentially local. In France, there was not one such station. So almost everyone was surprised when a national all-news channel, France-Infos, was founded in 1987 and proved popular, soon attracting over 8 percent of the cumulative audience. Even its creator, Roland Faure, then head of the state-owned Radio-France, expected only about 3 percent; his idea had consisted simply of making better use of the journalistic resources of the existing Radio-France networks. France-Infos is like the typical U.S. all-news station except that it deals only with national and world news and can be heard 24 hours a day by almost all of the 55 million people in the country. And, of course, there are no barking interruptions by irrelevant advertisers. The average listening time is short, but France-Infos reaches the elite. In 1993, it seemed the only such national radio on earth.

And now for the two octopuses. As mentioned before, from the 1940s to the 1970s, the purpose of the *Société financière de radiodiffusion* (SOFIRAD) was to manage the French state's shares in peripheral radios serving the French audience. What the SOFIRAD does now is quite different. Today it holds the state's shares in 40-odd companies that are engaged in developing, feeding and running commercial radio stations operating far from France for non-French-speaking audiences. With its 15 stations serving 40 million listeners, it complements Radio France International (RFI), the noncommercial Voice of France.

The first station started by SOFIRAD is known as "RMC Middle East" or Radio Monte Carlo, with studios in Paris and its 600-kw (soon to be 1,200-kw) AM transmitters in Cyprus. It became the second most-listened to foreign station in the region; in 1993 in Saudi Arabia, its 11.4 rating exceeded that of the BBC.

The next station, established in 1980, was Radio Méditerrannée Internationale (Médi 1) in Tangiers, set up in cooperation with the Moroccan state to serve the former French colonies of the Maghreb and West Africa, using two languages, colloquial Arabic and French, and the easy, dynamic style that made Europe No. 1 so popular in France in the 1950s and '60s.

The next year came Africa No. 1, built in central Africa, with a majority participation of the government of Gabon. It is now listened to in the whole of francophone black Africa, even as far north as Mali. Listening is made all the easier as its shortwave broadcasts are relayed on FM in a number of major cities, such as Cotonou, Abidjan and Dakar, and in Paris because of its large immigrant population. More recently, Radio Caribbean International (RCI) was launched, and closer to home, an FM station in Lisbon using French and Portuguese.

The SOFIRAD is also active now in Eastern Europe in cooperation with both Europe No. 1 (Europa Plus stations in Moscow and St. Petersburg, with affiliates in Nijni-Novgorod, Samara, etc.) and with the French network Radio Nostalgie, a subsidiary of RMC that since 1992 has broadcast 24 hours a day in Moscow and St. Petersburg.

The second media conglomerate is the Compagnie Luxembourgeoise de Télédiffusion (CLT), one of the largest media groups in Europe, born in 1933 when Radio Luxembourg (RTL) began broadcasting programs in French, German and, later, English. Its originality is that, though it belongs to Belgian and, mainly, French interests, it is rooted in a very small principality, Luxembourg. From that independent base, it serves most nations in northern Europe in their own languages. It is a truly multinational company, as opposed to media groups like Fininvest (Berlusconi), which is clearly Italian, or the German Bertelsman.

As far as radio is concerned, the CLT is the No. 1 group in Europe. In France particularly, RTL is the most popular radio station, with a 19 percent "cume" in 1993, or 8 million regular listeners), and the CLT is reaching ever more listeners through the creation of new networks and stations (e.g., the M 40 network, in cooperation with SER, the Spanish broadcaster) and the acquisition of others.

In Germany, the CLT was no longer doing well because of competition from newly created local and regional private stations. So now it syndicates music and news programs to the upstarts, buys into them and obtains permission to operate local channels itself, as in Berlin or Stuttgart. It is doing the same in Belgium, where Bel RTL has become the No. 1 private generalist station, and in the Netherlands, for which RTL Radio was launched in 1992. The CLT also owns RTL Prague.

Even Britons, during the BBC's austere pre-World War II era, often listened to Radio Luxembourg, at least on Sundays. But as that program did less well against the BBC, the CLT started a peripheral station in Ireland called Atlantic 252, aimed at Britain. More recently, Britain seems to have lost its talent for developing electronic media systems so original and satisfactory (or at least fervently admired, like Channel 4) that they were imitated the world over from Sweden to Australia and from Japan to Germany.

In the United States, many radio stations succeed beautifully in achieving their sole object: making money. This, in the eyes of some Europeans, they achieve by prostituting themselves to any layer of society they find profitable. Only American Public Radio and National Public Radio, the nonprofit networks, seem to pay any attention to serving the public with such programs as NPR's "All Things Considered" or APR's "Prairie Home Companion."

That, of course, is a caricature. By no stretch of the imagination could anyone regard Anglo-American radio as being worthless. But I wish to highlight the fact that no survey of radio, the most transnational of media, can ignore the vast proportion of it that is not Anglo-American. Radio certainly is a "forgotten medium" but, insofar as many U.S. observers are concerned, what is forgotten about radio is that part of it which operates outside Britain and the United States.

Claude-Jean Bertrand is a media scholar and professor in the Institut français de presse et des sciences de l'information at the Université de Paris-2.

13

The BBC—From Maiden Aunt
to Sexy Upstart

Asa Briggs

"Suddenly," a British journalist recently observed, "the wireless is a red-hot sexy medium? For years it was the maiden aunt of broadcasting, but now there are superstars and household names crawling over dear little steam radio, just panting to start up their own station."

In Britain, the people now panting to start up radio stations are taking advantage of the opening up of radio channels to competitive bidding. Some of the bidders have worked inside the BBC. A generation ago, however, during the 1960s when the BBC retained its radio monopoly, it was the BBC that found it necessary to argue the case for radio, identifying what it *could* do and what it *should* do. The BBC lost its television monopoly in 1955, but it continued to broadcast in both media, and those of its staff who were still working in radio felt they were competing with their own colleagues in television.

There were signs, nonetheless, of a "maiden aunt" mentality. There was a serious debate about the future of radio, which few people in the BBC, whatever their views, would have dismissed as "dear little steam radio." The term "steam radio" had already come into fashion but was not much used inside the BBC even after television began to count for a major proportion of BBC expenditures after 1958.

The BBC's public pronouncements on the subject of radio were stirring, and they remain relevant (although no one could have called them "sexy"). The most controversial document in the BBC's history, *Broadcasting in the Seventies*, published in 1969, was about radio, not television. "The role of radio cannot be judged in isolation," it recognized. "There are still some fields for which it has a unique role, but it has to live with the other mass media, above all with television.... It should not be 'trendy' in the pejorative sense, but it should certainly be relevant." It is even more illuminating that such public documents were published inside the BBC. Without any other evidence, they prove that the BBC was never a monopolistic organization. They deserve to be disinterred at a time when the future of radio is being discussed again in a new setting.

One contribution to the discussion, neither completely public nor completely private, was a lecture delivered in March 1964 by the BBC's then-recently appointed director of sound broadcasting, Frank Gillard. He began by quoting from a 1959 article that had appeared in the *BBC Quarterly,* a prestigious publication, long since dead. "The first casualty of television, possibly the only casualty," a senior official in the BBC had written then, "is not the local cinema or the country theatre: it is sound radio." That particular prophet, Gillard observed, had long faded from the scene. Sound radio, in this "almost fully arrived television age, is thriving and still full of promise," he said. Its daily audience had been rising steadily, with audience increases each year—indeed, it was only one-fifth below that of television—and radio sets were outselling televisions in the shops. As far as public attention was concerned, the BBC received more letters in relation to radio than in relation to television.

Gillard believed that the continuing power of radio depended on the fact it was being supplied along with television by the same provider, a provider with "40 years of responsible development" behind it. And he contrasted Britain with those countries where radio had been degraded to "the status of an amplified juke-box," whose major function was "to grind out the Top Twenty hour by hour." Even so, he was impressed by American local radio and vigorously led the campaign inside and outside the BBC to introduce BBC local radio to Britain during the later 1960s. Local radio stations would "tell the running daily story of local life" and "stimulate every citizen's interest in local affairs," he maintained. They could also play a major part in "the immense programme of educational broadcasting which is now interestingly called for in Britain." On the importance of radio in the educational advance of the 1960s, Gillard was right, although it was national radio, not local radio, that was to prove of key importance in the work of Britain's Open University, which enrolled its first students in 1971. Significantly, it had first been called the "University of the Air" and all the stress was on television, but its first Planning Committee attached as much value to the use of radio time as it did to television.

Radio, as Gillard noted, was "relatively cheap and simple," while television was "costly and cumbrous." An hour of television in 1964 cost nearly eight times as much as an hour of radio. There were then three BBC radio channels and one television channel and it was radio that was catering to minorities. Radio was changing in approach, however. Its peak listening hours were at times when television screens were blank (there was no breakfast television in Britain). It also devoted far more attention to news; indeed, in Britain, the switch to "topicality" during the 1960s was as prominent in broadcasting as the switch to television.

There was also an emphasis on music across the spectrum, from Promenade Concerts to Top of the Pops. A new music program was launched in 1964. It had a high proportion of live music, more than a half (in Britain, the use of gramophone record—"needletime"—was severely restricted) and the BBC was the country's major patron of music. All this was positive. Yet in the Gillard regime, there were to be radio casualties also. Talks of a formal kind, a well established BBC genre, declined in importance. "Features," which claimed to be a radio art form, ceased to be produced in a separate BBC department. Above all, the concept of balanced daily programs offering a wide variety of cultural fare disappeared in favor of what was called "generic radio," with three (later four) different radio channels appealing to target audiences.

Traditional BBC fare, promoted originally under the commanding influence of John Reith, the first BBC director-general, had maneuvered listeners, in Gillard's phrase, "by subtle and cunning planning devices" to listen to things "which they would normally never dream of switching on." Gillard said, "At a peak evening hour, a poetry programme or a recital of camouflaged chamber music or some educational lecture could be 'cradled'—that was our word for it—between two highly popular variety shows." And people did not switch off. Now they did. The new radio policy, therefore, was "to offer in straightforward fashion, without guile or cunning, the widest possible range of output on a consistent, predictable planning basis," Gillard said. "Each individual then knows exactly where to go for what he wants. He can easily find his way about the programmes, and he can build up his own personal habits of listening."

This note of confidence in 1964 was to be threatened inside the BBC during the next five years when it became abundantly clear that the British government was unwilling to set a license fee high enough to sustain radio as Gillard conceived of it, let alone provide adequate funds for the development of a new local radio system. And there was another challenge to the whole BBC conception of radio when radio pirates, broadcasting from off the British coast, attracted sizable audiences, mainly but not exclusively young, for programs consisting of pop music and chat. The first pirate pop station, Radio Caroline, went on the air for the first time in March 1964. It was followed by others and it took laborious efforts to introduce and carry legislation to force the pirates off the air in August 1967. The Marine &c. Broadcasting Offences Act was carried only after the British government had decided to introduce a public service substitute and after the Conservative Party publicly favored the creation of commercial local radio.

The BBC did not drown the pirates. It signed them on, beginning a new Radio 1 service consisting largely of the same kind of fare that the pirates had provided offshore, acquiring more "needletime" than it had hitherto at its disposal. Its first program, introduced by "jingles," new to the BBC, was presented by one of the first pirate disc jockeys, Tony Blackburn, who received a message of congratulations from the BBC's old continental radio rival, Radio Luxembourg. On this occasion, the maiden aunt image was used at least by one critic. For George Melly, this was "Auntie's first freak out."

It was what happened to the BBC's three other radio channels that marked the further triumph of "generic radio." They were now numbered 2, 3 and 4. Gillard had always thought that the "Home Service," the old BBC name for what now became mainstream Radio 4, had been absurd. "All broadcasting is a home service," he argued. "Why tack it on to just one channel?" Few people were bothered about the absurdity, and the service, which now actually increased its audience as a result of improved news programs, continued to be called "Radio 4, the Home Service" for another two years.

By then, two further major enquiries into the future of radio had been carried out. The first of them, a Working Group on the Future of Radio, reported in January 1969, overlapping towards the end of its labors with the second, a smaller Policy Study Group, which was primarily concerned with making savings and which set out the options that the Board of Management and, finally, the Board of Governors had to choose between before publication of the plan for the future, *Broadcasting in the Seventies.*

The representations made by radio producers, some of them highly talented, to the Working Group were varied both in approach and conclusions. One, at least, believed that "the days of public service broadcasting" were over and that "commercial radio" was likely to come, "whatever attempts we may make to avoid it." BBC radio would then benefit in "exactly the same way" as television had benefited. Another thought that such talk showed lack of confidence: "We appear to accept all the conceits and assertions of the opposition"; for him, all radio and television advertisements were "gratuitous, ethereal litter, worse than junk mail." Some favored a separate news channel, which a generation later was to become BBC policy: one of the unconvinced called it "broiler house journalism,...unable to lift its sight much beyond the next half-hour segment." A significant number pressed for a separate channel to be devoted to education of all kinds. One of the most radical witnesses would have abolished Radio 4 and substituted for it various forms of market-related national, regional and local radio, abolishing the whole concept of a great national audience in the process. Some wanted a switch to VHF/FM; others resisted it. Some favored advertising, limited or unlimited; others would rather have resigned. One objected to using the press and television, "more primitive and vastly expensive media," to campaign for a higher BBC license fee; one observed (without, as he said, any help from Marshall McLuhan) that he had come to the conclusion that "radio is in all circumstances a less complete medium of communication, a smaller entity than television."

Offered such a range of opinions, the Working Group would have accepted advertising as the last resort, if all campaigning for a higher license fee had failed. There was a minimum range of service that the BBC could offer the public. Radio 1, however, had to stay, whatever happened. Radio 1 might have been "the product of muddled thinking" by the government after it had been confronted with the pirates, but to scrap it would be to isolate the BBC from "the youthful section of its audience and to throw the door open for a competitor." Radio 3 could not be scrapped either, though it had the smallest audience and presented the most costly programs. It incorporated the old Third Program—the cultural program—which had been hailed in the post-war years as the jewel in BBC's crown. Small though its audience was, it included "those who are most vocal and most influential." Radio 4 occupied "a unique position at the center"—"It's complete excision," despite the thoughts of the one radical critic of it, was "unthinkable," Radio 2 which offered light music and undemanding fare for an older audience than Radio 1, might "superficially give the impression of being old-fashioned and of dwindling importance," but the audience for it was of strategic importance to the BBC: "If properly served, it would stay loyal to the BBC in face of competition."

Strongly defending "generic radio" but refraining from endorsing either a news channel or a new channel devoted exclusively to music, the Working Group ended as positively as Gillard had done in his 1964 lecture. Having asked itself the question as to whether the BBC, still in its monopolistic position, was providing more radio "than was really needed," the answer was unequivocally no. Radio was there to stay. There were few references in the report to mobile radio or to "background listening." There were references, however, to better management, a theme which was to figure prominently in all future BBC inquiries. There were also signs that "producer power," a main theme of the 1970s (largely in relation to television) was already being discussed in Broadcasting House. One witness urged "improving the structure of our organization so that the producer is fully engaged, fully stretched, largely independent and much more efficient."

Only inside a large public broadcasting organization like the BBC could the debate about the future of radio have been handled in this way. The market would have tested choices and settled them in quite different fashion. Still, BBC radio did survive and flourish, maintaining a distinct set of identities and serving, in the words of Charles Curran, the BBC's director-general of the late 1960s, as the "medium of choice." "Radio is where people choose what they want to listen to," he said.

The policy study group generally favored the pattern of radio broadcasting that the Working Group had outlined. Since it was called upon to suggest cost reductions, however, it had to focus on difficult choices, suggesting, for example, which of the BBC's orchestras should be disbanded and which wavelength changes were essential if a full generic radio plan was adopted. One suggested change was that Radio 3 should lose its medium-wave frequency and switch entirely to VHF/FM, which was bound to provoke public controversy. There was bound to be conflict also on effects of changes to regional broadcasting. There were six BBC regions, and while the national regions—Scotland, Wales and Northern Ireland—would continue to enjoy a substantial degree of devolution, the three English regions would lose ground. Local radio would, in effect, act as a substitute for regional radio. *Broadcasting in the Seventies* did not explain, however, how the changes were to be financed, and it required a compromise deal between the government and the BBC to find an answer in the month after the document appeared: The music cuts were reduced; the government agreed to increase the license fee. The BBC could go ahead with a plan for 40 local radio stations.

The compromise did not dispel public controversy. A new organization, the Campaign for Better Broadcasting, attacked the BBC's "New Deal," drawing on the support of a wide range of powerful national figures. If the BBC were to go ahead with generic broadcasting on the lines that had been suggested, this, it was claimed, would be "disastrous to standards of quality and public service broadcasting" and would seriously threaten "the unique role of the BBC." It was a mistake to segregate people into classes on the assumption that "there are large numbers of people who like only one program." The name of Reith was now directly involved and, in retrospect, this campaign stands out as the last campaign to maintain BBC radio as it had been on the eve of the advent of television. What the critics, however distinguished, failed to examine, which the BBC itself had tried to do, was the consequence for radio of the development of a huge television audience.

It was because the BBC had made a real effort to understand the dynamics that, despite the *furore*, the new radio pattern was accepted quickly. Nonetheless, the BBC as an institution was never thereafter entirely secure. It had lost the support of some of the most influential figures in the British life and culture. The fact that they were as divided on as many key points as the internal critics of the plan were did not matter. Whatever line they took, they felt there had been a surrender. It was chronologically fitting that Lord Reith died in the summer of 1971. He belonged to an earlier generation than most of them.

Asa Briggs, Lord Briggs of Lewes, a preeminent historian of modern communications and a 1987–88 senior fellow at The Freedom Forum Media Studies Center, is completing the fifth volume of A History of Broadcasting in the United Kingdom. *Former provost of Worcester College, Oxford, he is chancellor of the Open University.*

14

Devoted to "Auntie Beeb"

Suzanne Levy

The British public had its knickers in a twist.

The calming inevitability of Life As We Know It was under attack—BBC Radio was about to shift its schedules. The usual background hum of the chattering classes swelled to a primal scream; institutions in Britain are *not* tampered with lightly. The subject was dissected at dinner parties, addressed in newspaper editorials and even reached Parliament, where a motion was planned to prevent this unthinkable occurrence.

And what was causing this particular furor? "Woman's Hour," a popular radio program that had aired faithfully at 2 p.m. for the past 40 years, was to be moved to 10:30 a.m. Even worse—its name was to be changed! Was *nothing* sacred?

A little context is needed, perhaps. The British have had an intimate relationship with BBC Radio for most of this century, beginning in 1922. It carried the country through World War II, informing, educating and entertaining with classical music, drama, documentaries, half-hour comedies and "Children's Hour." BBC Radio is to Britain as Mom and apple pie is to the States. Not lightly is it called "Auntie Beeb."

The network closest to people's hearts, perhaps, is BBC's Radio 4, the national speech and arts channel. (The other national networks, Radios 1, 2, 3 and 5, broadcast pop, light music, classical music and sports/education, respectively.)

Radio 4 is the BBC at its most eclectic, and it has a fiercely loyal audience, who love it as much for its eccentricity as for its substance and depth. Unlike radio in the United States (with the possible exception of National Public Radio and American Public Radio), Radio 4 has

developed a role at the center of British intellectual life. Hosts and producers who "escape" Radio 4 for television often return sheepishly, con-
fessing how much they missed the intelligence of the network.

Radio 4 is perhaps the purest practitioner of the ethos introduced by
John Reith, the BBC's first director-general, who maintained that the
broadcasting system should give the public what it needs, not necessarily what it wants, "because very few people know what they want and
even fewer what they need."

During a typical day, Radio 4 might dish up a debate on whether an
author's work can be admired if his or her personal life is despicable;
radio drama with current leading theatrical names (including many from
Hollywood—Richard Dreyfuss and Kathleen Turner recently gave up
huge fees to record at the BBC); and a 45-minute exploration of the
politics of abortion.

Yet there are more plebian pursuits too: "Gardener's Question Time"
is hugely popular, as are lunchtime quiz shows and comedy programs.

In fact, for comedy, radio's lower costs can mean more risk taking;
innovative Radio 4 shows have often crossed over into television, becoming wildly successful. The comedy-improv TV show "Whose Line
Is It Anyway," shown in the United States on PBS and Comedy Central,
started life on a late-night Radio 4 comedy slot.

At other times there are whole hordes of public affairs shows—on the
arts, food, consumer affairs, disabled issues, travel and holidays along with
well-informed call-in shows, where the level of debate is surprisingly high.

"Woman's Hour," the program whose proposed time shift produced
such national angst, is a unique show that has evolved with its audience.
Begun in 1946, it gave housewives a chance to put their feet up after
lunch; today it's a mainstream magazine show with a feminist edge,
focusing on anything of interest to women—celebrity interviews, political discussions, beautifully crafted features and a daily serial, ranging
from "Jane Eyre" to "V.I. Warshawski."

Moving "Woman's Hour" prompted outrage because listeners feared
any tampering could mean its death; its particular worldview is vulnerable to criticism. And such labor-intensive, high-quality radio does not
come cheap. In an age when money's tight, this type of program could
be the first to go.

The spine of Radio 4 is its substantial news strand, running through
the day. But it's the morning news show —"Today"—that is the jewel in

Radio 4's crown. As the new day starts, 3 million listeners tune in to hear the stories on that day's political, economic and social agenda; breakfast television has never been able to break its hold. By refusing to pander to pressures to leaven the load, "Today" has maintained both popularity and prestige—for its devoted audience, it would be unthinkable to wake up without it.

It aims high, too, snaring interviews daily with top politicians and decisionmakers who are aware of its influence and appear, uncomplainingly, at 7:15 a.m. to explain their latest actions. "Today" often sets the news agenda for television and newspapers.

For up-and-coming politicians, it's also a prime time to show off one's nimble communication skills: Mrs. Thatcher, it was said, listened closely, and junior members of Parliament would lobby to be interviewed to demonstrate their potential to their beloved leader.

Even the highest strata of British society claim Radio 4 as its own. During the Persian Gulf war, Radio 4 experimented with an all-news network—nicknamed "Scud FM" by its weary workers. Afterwards, the country's news junkies enthused over the experience and a permanent channel was planned, on the old-fashioned long-wave wavelength, leaving Radio 4 to FM. But Radio 4's executives had overlooked the wrath of some listeners—those who disliked FM's sometimes spotty signal, technophobes who refused to progress to FM radios and those who lived outside its range.

Among the latter was Prince Charles, who publicly disclosed that he'd written to Marmaduke Hussey, the BBC chairman, to raise a concerned regal eyebrow. Apparently he listens to Radio 4 long wave whilst gardening on the most far-flung corners of the Queen's Scottish estate, Balmoral. How could he dally with his dahlias without Radio 4 to keep him company?

Coming soon after the "Woman's Hour" episode, stiff upper lips began to tremble. Outrage was heard in the English heartland, unleashing a "Save Radio 4 LW" campaign—10,000 letters of complaint, protesters descending on Broadcasting House. Incandescent expatriates organized demonstrations in Brussels, Dublin and Paris, but to no avail. An all-news network, it was announced, would go ahead. Prince Charles would have to sulk in silence.

So much anguish, so little cause? Perhaps a perceptive public had seen the future and rejected it—the encroachment of U.S.-style down-market format radio. (Stories are plentiful in Britain of Howard Stern and Rush Limbaugh's daily degradations.)

Radio 4 is a tastings menu of the finest restaurant—a little of this, a little of that—and you never know what the chef will recommend next. Serendipity enhances the pleasure. Deregulation already encourages introduction of more commercial light music, jazz, talk and minority stations, putting such a spread at risk from commercial nibblers.

To American ears, accustomed to FM and talk radio, Radio 4 is a strange creature—slow-paced, slightly stuffy and sometimes unbearably worthy. It attracts those criticisms in Britain, too, often accused of being overly white and middle class, focusing on older, suburban listeners.

But its listeners nevertheless continue to be passionate about it, with an almost proprietary zeal. Radio 4's boss, Michael Green, has learned to make changes with care, often quoting a letter he received from a listener upon taking over the network: "Congratulations on your new job. May I remind you, however, that you are merely the temporary custodian of my network. Tamper with it at your peril."

(Footnote: "Woman's Hour" *was* moved to 10:30 a.m. But it kept its name. Some things *are* sacred.)

Suzanne Levy, a 1992–93 research fellow at The Freedom Forum Media Studies Center and a radio producer in the BBC's New York bureau, formerly produced the BBC radio magazine "Woman's Hour."

15

Heating Up Clandestine Radio After the Cold War

Lawrence Soley

As the Cold War in Europe escalated in the late 1940s and the Greek civil war heated up, a mysterious voice came from nowhere over the shortwave band. "The Greek people [now] have their own powerful radio station—the Voice of Truth," the voice announced. The Voice of Truth began its twice-daily transmissions just after midnight on July 17, 1947, denouncing the U.S.-backed Greek government and its allies as monarcho-fascists guilty of war crimes.

On April 27, 1959, the CIA's radio monitoring unit, the Foreign Broadcast Information Service, got its first taste of the Farsi-language National Voice of Iran, which began its broadcast life by condemning the Shah of Iran and his Western allies—principally the United States—as fascists.

The Voice of Truth and the National Voice of Iran were just two of many clandestine stations broadcasting from the communist bloc during the Cold War era. Although the Voice of Truth claimed to originate from liberated territory in Greece, it was actually based in Albania, moving to Romania in 1958; the National Voice of Iran broadcast from Baku in the Soviet Union. And there were others—Ce Soir en France, Oggi in Italia, Radio España Independiente, Radio Free Portugal, the Voice of the Turkish Communist Party, Our Radio (to Turkey), and German Freedom Station 904 (broadcasting from East to West Germany). None ever disclosed that their transmitters were in the Soviet bloc. Clandestine stations typically mislead listeners about their location, sponsorship and purpose.

For example, Radio Swan, an anti-Castro station that broadcast before and after the failed Bay of Pigs invasion, claimed to be private and commercial but was actually operated by the CIA; Soviet-based Radio España Independiente called itself "the Pyrenees radio station," implying that it was broadcasting from inside Spain.

There are three varieties of radio propaganda stations, of which two are clandestine. "White" stations are above-ground (not clandestine) operations that are truthful about their purposes and locations—Radio Free Europe and Radio Liberty, for example. "Gray" clandestine stations are operated by or attributed to indigenous dissident groups, such as Radio España Independiente and Voice of the Turkish Communist Party, which were in fact Soviet-sponsored and located in the Soviet bloc. "Black" clandestine station broadcasts masquerade as stations sponsored by an enemy. During the Vietnam war, for example, the CIA occasionally operated a black clandestine station that claimed to be Liberation Radio, the Viet Cong's gray station.

Ironically, the easing of Cold War tensions and the spread of democracy in Eastern Europe and elsewhere have not meant fewer clandestine radio operations but more. Although most communist-inspired or Soviet-backed stations went off the air after Presidents Reagan and Gorbachev ended the Cold War, clandestine radio traffic worldwide has increased since then, perhaps one manifestation of unleashed nationalism and demands for political democracy. Overall, more clandestine stations broadcast today than during the early 1980s as regional political struggles use clandestine radio to press their causes and attack their enemies. Some of these—such as stations broadcasting to Angola, Mozambique and Afghanistan—have their roots in the Cold War, but their continued operation indicates that many conflicts once portrayed as East-West confrontations were in fact principally indigenous conflicts in which the superpowers became embroiled. In Angola and Afghanistan, as was the case with many civil wars, the conflicts are primarily tribal or ethnic rather than ideological. Although ideology often was used to mask the ethnic nature of the conflicts, they served as convenient vehicles for U.S.-Soviet geopolitical maneuvering.

Many Soviet-backed and communist-inspired clandestine stations went off the air during the mid-1970s with the fall of authoritarian regimes in Portugal, Spain and Greece. Radio Free Portugal made its last broadcast in October 1974 after the military ousted Marcello Caetano.

Greece's Voice of Truth signed-off in 1975 after a military junta was replaced by civilian leader Constantine Karamanlis. These communist vehicles saw their battles as having been won. In 1977, with the death of Francisco Franco and the legalization of Spain's Communist Party (PCE), Radio España Independiente ended 36 years of clandestine broadcasts when it declared its "mission has been accomplished. In a way, in wiping out the last vestiges of a clandestine existence that we never wanted, but which was imposed on us by the fascist dictatorship, the PCE is giving, as if it were necessary, further proof of its wishes to abide by the democratic game." Ironically, the PCE then splintered into factions and became less influential than during Franco's time; other Western European communist parties also declined in size and strength since the 1970s.

Other Soviet-sponsored clandestine stations that survived into the 1980s were eventually shut down by Mikhail Gorbachev, who closed the last such stations broadcasting to Europe—Voice of the Turkish Communist Party and its sister station, Our Radio—in 1987-88. Since the dissolution of the Soviet Union, no clandestine stations have broadcast from Russia, although Radio Moscow now carries anti-Marxist programming directed at Vietnam and Ethiopia, two former Soviet allies. The only Marxist clandestine stations remaining on the air in the post-Cold War era are operated by groups with few direct ties to the former Eastern bloc, broadcasting to countries with highly repressive governments. The Radio of the Sudanese People's Liberation Army (Radio SPLA) still broadcasts against the Islamic fundamentalist government in Khartoum, and the Voice of the Sarbedaran transmits anti-government messages to Iran on behalf of the Union of Iranian Communists.

Radio SPLA typifies Marxist stations that have survived into the post-Cold War era. During the 10-year Sudanese civil war that began in the 1980s, the SPLA was backed by Ethiopia, a Soviet client state, rather than directly by Moscow. But this was not a communist-inspired struggle. Although SPLA leader John Garang and his followers claimed to be Marxists, the war pitted Christians and animists from the South against Islamic northerners, who attempted to force Islamic law on the whole nation. Radio SPLA broadcast from Addis Ababa from 1984 until May 27, 1991, the day before Tigrean rebels entered the Ethiopian capital, returning to the air in October 1991 from southern Sudan.

A society's lack of openness is the surest predictor that clandestine stations will appear, whether the nondemocratic government is a military junta, communist or capitalist. Since the ouster of President Jean-Bertrand Aristide, for instance, a pro-Aristide station has broadcast to Haiti; Algerian fundamentalists started La Radio de la Fidelité after the government canceled runoff elections that the fundamentalists were expected to win, and several anti-government stations resurfaced in Burma following the military's refusal to hold promised elections. With the end of right-wing, authoritarian governments, the Marxist clandestine stations that opposed them also disappeared, although many of these stations have been replaced by anti-communist transmitters opposing the governments of Cuba, China, Vietnam and Laos, and by clandestine stations operated by separatist ethnic groups.

Like its old foe the Soviet Union, the United States sponsored or covertly funded many clandestine stations during the Cold War era, broadcasting to Guatemala, Cuba, China, Iran, Southeast Asia, Poland, Afghanistan and Nicaragua, among others. The CIA-sponsored Guatemalan station, Voice of Liberation, for example, was instrumental in the 1954 ouster of the democratically-elected but left-leaning President Jacobo Arbenz, who was replaced with a right-wing military government.

Southeast Asia was a particularly fertile ground for American propaganda initiatives from the 1950s onward. In Vietnam, U.S.-sponsored broadcasts aimed at destabilizing the North began almost as soon as the French signed the Geneva Accords and continued throughout the Vietnam war. Even after U.S. withdrawal and the signing of the 1973 Agreement on Ending the Fighting and Restoring Peace in Vietnam, new anti-communist clandestine stations cropped up. In *Decent Interval*, Frank Snepp noted that Henry Kissinger "directed the CIA to set up a clutch of 'gray' propaganda stations to harass the North Vietnamese and Viet Cong." These stations—two aimed at Cambodia and three at Vietnam—broadcast from "House 7," a secret communications complex named for its address at No. 7 Hong Thap Tu Street in Saigon. Clandestine stations continue to operate in Southeast Asia. Following communist takeovers in Laos, Cambodia and Vietnam, a series of anti-communist stations went on the air, most sponsored by exile groups based in the United States with the tacit approval of the American government.

The Vietnamese government also sponsored a station that attacked the Khmer Rouge immediately before its December 1978 invasion of Cambodia; after its ouster from Phnom Penh, the Khmer Rouge responded with two of its own stations, which harried the Vietnameseinstalled Cambodian government. In October 1991, the Khmer Rouge stations merged, creating the Voice of the Great National United Front of Cambodia, still in operation. On the other side is another gray station, the Voice of the Khmer, covertly funded by the United States in support of deposed Prince Norodom Sihanouk, although it was silenced this year pending the outcome of the United Nations-supervised elections.

During the 1980s, the United States set up stations that broadcast against the pro-Soviet governments of Poland, Afghanistan and Nicaragua, funded with monies channeled through the National Endowment for Democracy, a quasi-governmental agency established by Congress to fund pro-Western political groups. In Afghanistan, the mujahedeen operated several U.S.-backed clandestine stations during the Afghan civil war. Islamic fundamentalist Hezb-i Islami group still operates Radio Message of Freedom. The group is headed by Prime Minister-designate Gulbuddin Hekmatyar, who shelled Kabul after the fall of the communist government in an April 1992 power struggle that killed tens of thousands, most of them civilians. In Nicaragua, the contras' 50,000-watt Radio Liberación—its birth announced at a 1987 press conference by Elliott Abrams, then U.S. assistant secretary of state for inter-American affairs—signed off after Violeta Chamorro was elected president in democratic elections in 1990.

Since the end of the Cold War, however, while the Soviet-backed clandestine radio efforts have largely disappeared, the United States has continued to sponsor such stations. Two prominent examples targeted Panama's Gen. Manuel Noriega and Iraq's Saddam Hussein.

The first anti-Noriega station appeared shortly after President Reagan considered a plan in April 1988 to beam clandestine broadcasts into Panama from a blimp or a ship off shore. Noriega's Panama Defense Forces (PDF) charged that Radio Constitucional broadcasts originated in the Canal Zone, a violation of the Panama Canal treaty, and were directed by the CIA; the United States denied the charge, blaming backers of deposed President Eric Arturo Delvalle. Regardless, the station signal was so weak that most Panamanians were unable to receive it. By December, another gray U.S.-backed anti-Noriega station was on the air. The Voice of Freedom claimed to be operated by the Armed Liberation Forces of Hugo Spadafora (FLASH), named for a Noriega opponent decapitated near the Panama-Costa Rica border in 1985, although Noriega again accused the United States. There was, in fact, a guerrilla group called FLASH, composed of Panamanian dissidents, Nicaraguan contras and Costa Rican soldiers of fortune. When the United States invaded Panama in December 1989, FLASH seized key installations near the Costa Rican border. Although they disarmed Panamanian traffic police, American troops let FLASH guerrillas keep their weapons. U.S. officials told the *New York Times* that FLASH cooperated with the U.S. Army but was not on the payroll.

But another anti-Noriega station, the Voice of Liberty, has been even more closely tied to the U.S. government than either Radio Constitucional or Voice of Freedom. Beginning in 1989, its programs featured speeches of exiled Panamanians in the United States, who denounced Noriega and encouraged protests in favor of democracy. Like Radio Constitucional, however, Voice of Liberty had an almost inaudible signal; in Panama, the joke went, Voice of Liberty was so clandestine that it couldn't be heard.

Panamanian authorities arrested a U.S. citizen, Kurt Frederick Muse, claiming that Muse, whose wife worked for the U.S. Defense Department, had confessed to operating the station; Muse was reported to have stored $350,000-worth of radio transmission equipment in seven Panama City apartments. Although the United States denied employing Muse, his jail was one of the first buildings seized by U.S. troops when they invaded Panama in 1989, and Muse was whisked back to Washington, prompting Bob Woodward to conclude in *The Commanders* that Muse had indeed been a CIA operative.

If U.S. clandestine stations in Panama failed to foment rebellion or even to generate much listenership, broadcasts aimed at Saddam Hussein during the Persian Gulf war succeeded too well, only to be bungled at the end. The U.S.-sponsored anti-Saddam station generated widespread listenership among northern Kurds and southern Shiites and eventually helped ignite a rebellion against the regime in Baghdad following Desert Storm. But when the Kurds and Shiites rose against Saddam, as the United States had urged, President Bush and allied troops wouldn't help them, and the rebels were crushed by Iraqi troops.

The clandestine Voice of Free Iraq made its first broadcast from Saudi Arabia on Jan. 2, 1991, describing Saddam Hussein as a crook and a mad bull who should be overthrown. Subsequently renamed, the clandestine Voice of the Iraqi People is managed by Ibrahim al-Zubaidi, a former director of Baghdad Radio, and Salah Omar Ali, a relative of

Hussein who was the Iraqi minister of information during the 1980s. During the Gulf war, its programs were produced by 40 Iraqi exiles in a complex protected by Saudi troops in Jidda, on the Saudi coast.

In the face of criticism that followed the failure of the Shiite and Kurdish uprisings against Saddam Hussein, officials in the Bush administration, while not confirming that the Voice of the Iraqi People was U.S.-sponsored, said the station had never promised the rebels assistance and had called mainly for a military coup. But as late as April 6, 1991, the Voice of the Iraqi People broadcast: "Brother Iraqis, sons of our people, builders of civilizations, Baghdad is the jewel and the mother of knowledge, literature and art.... Baghdad calls you. Baghdad calls its sons, its men, its lovers. Baghdad, that haven of peace, has been mutilated by Saddam.... Protect it from the claws of the filthy clique. Save it. Save the mother of Iraq. Reward Baghdad by rebelling."

Firiad Hiwaizi, a Kurdish exile who recorded programs for the Voice of the Iraqi People, later bitterly regretted encouraging a rebellion that was so bloodily suppressed. "I feel guilty now," Hiwaizi told the *Washington Post*, "because I'm sure a lot of people died because of my advice."

Besides the Voice of the Iraqi People, five other regionally based stations call for Hussein's ouster—two Kurdish stations and three originating from neighboring Iran. The Kurdish Democratic Party, headed by Massoud Barzani, has operated the Voice of Iraqi Kurdistan intermittently since 1965, and Jalal Talabani's Patriotic Union of Kurdistan operates Voice of the People of Kurdistan, which has broadcast irregularly since 1988, and directed Voice of the Iraqi Revolution in the early 1980s. Both Kurdish groups have received U.S. assistance.

The Iranian anti-Iraq stations are Voice of the Islamic Revolution in Iraq, Voice of Rebellious Iraq, and Voice of the Disavowal of the Polytheists. The first, speaking for the pro-Iranian Islamic Assembly of the Islamic Revolution in Iraq (SAIRI), appeared in December 1980, three months after Iraq invaded Iran. Its broadcasts ceased with normalization of Iran-Iraq relations in August 1990 but resurfaced in March 1991, when Iraqi Shiites rebelled in southern Iraq. The Voice of Rebellious Iran, first monitored in March 1991, carries programs supporting the SAIRI and refers to Saddam Hussein as "the tyrant" and his government as the "Saddamist gang." Often ridiculing Hussein's governing abilities, the station reported on May 31, 1991, that "the defeated tyrant Saddam

Hussein suffered a nervous breakdown in the wake of the liberation of Kuwait and the outbreak of popular unrest in Iraqi cities and villages...." The Iraqi government responded with its own clandestine radio stations— Holy Mecca Radio, which appeared in August 1990 and attacked the Saudi monarchy; and Voice of the Crusader, opposing Teheran's Islamic fundamentalist government (operated by the guerrilla group Mujahedeen al-Khalq, the station broadcast to Iran during the Iran-Iraq war but when Iran-Iraq relations were re-established in 1990, Iraq silenced the station as a gesture of goodwill and deported Iraq-based members of the mujahedeen to Iran, where they were executed).

Wherever authoritarian regimes, political conflict or civil wars exist, there is clandestine radio, a function of social strife and limits on open channels of free expression: Radio Vorgan—the Voice of Resistance of the Black Cockerel broadcasts to Angola, and Voice of the Oromo Liberation Front excoriates Ethiopia's new government. Many others broadcast to Africa—Sudan's Radio SPLA, Radio de la Fidelité in Algeria, Palipehutu Radio in Burundi, Rwanda's Radio Muhabara, Togo's Radio Liberty, Liberia's Radio Gbarnga, the Voice of Renamo in Mozambique and Western Sahara's Voice of Free Sahara; in Somalia, almost every warlord has a station or two. About the same number broadcast throughout Asia—in Burma, China, Taiwan, the Koreas, Laos, India, Cambodia, Vietnam and Sri Lanka.

The increase in regional ethnic conflicts around the world suggests that the number of clandestine stations also is likely to increase, despite the end of the Cold War and the dissolution of the Soviet bloc. In fact, clandestine broadcasts in the former Soviet Union have played an important role in ethnic conflicts there—Azerbaijani Radio Azadlyk (Radio Freedom), for instance, helped stir up conflict with neighboring Armenia.

Such electronic expression may be both a tool of covert political action by governments and an artifact of grassroots democracy. Use of clandestine radio has proven effective for governments against enemies in changing world and regional political equations, for superpowers in their geopolitical chess match and for indigenous political parties and splinter groups. All that's required to operate a clandestine radio station in support or opposition of one cause or another is a transmitter, a message and the hope that someone will listen. There is every indication they will continue to flourish, with or without a Cold War. And because radio can reach all segments of society regardless of education or socio-economic class, clandestine messages will continue to be the preferred medium for groups seeking to express their views or to foment revolution, liberation and rebellion.

Lawrence Soley, Colnik Chair of Communication at Marquette University, is author of Radio Warfare *and co-author of* Clandestine Radio Broadcasting.

IV

The Structure of Radio

16

Public Policy and Radio—
A Regulator's View

Andrew C. Barrett

During this decade, rapid advances in communications technologies will force the Federal Communications Commission (FCC) to assess constantly its rationale for regulating radio. Such traditional goals include concepts of ubiquitous local service and diversity of ownership to serve the varied segments of the U.S. population.

In the near future, digital technologies could enable broadcasters to transmit multiple channels of programming within narrower frequency bandwidths, or simultaneously to transmit multiple audio and data services within their present AM or FM bandwidths. Multichannel programming already is a reality in the world of television; such technical capabilities could alter the complexion of the radio industry. The importance of traditional broadcast policies, however, has not diminished. Free, over-the-air broadcasting remains a primary means of linking the common experiences of Americans in local communities throughout the United States.

Today, technological changes, combined with a difficult and prolonged recession, have made the pursuit of "diversity" and "localism" in broadcast policy more challenging than ever before. During the recession of the early 1990s, declining corporate revenues and extensive corporate restructuring reduced advertising revenues, the lifeblood of radio broadcast operations. This decline, in turn, forced many corporate advertisers to reassess their advertising budgets; ad spending by seven of the top 10 corporate advertisers was down in the early 1990s, reported Arbitron's *Media Watch.*

At the same time, corporate restructuring also increased the jobless rate. Because the unemployment rate hit lows in 1992 not reached since the Great Depression, consumer spending was correspondingly low, forcing advertisers to make more frugal choices. The radio industry did not escape the negative impact of these recessionary adjustments. Where jobs were lost or company operations closed, radio revenues felt the impact.

During the 1980s, "flash cut" deregulation at the FCC spurred fierce intra- and inter-industry competition. An increase in station allocations on the FM band between 1980 and 1991 resulted in 39 percent more FM stations; the increase in the number of AM stations was slightly less. Some regulators have attributed the poor economic condition of the industry to the oversaturation that resulted from this deregulation.

During that same period, the cable television industry grew and matured into a fierce competitor for advertising dollars. Television stations also increased in numbers and competed more aggressively for advertisers. The result—more media outlets chasing a limited supply of advertising revenue.

Deregulation, combined with the severe economic recession, had a harsh impact on the radio industry. Half of all stations lost money in 1990; 300 licensees went off the air and the growth rate of radio revenues dropped to 6 percent, down from 12 percent in the mid-1980s. Furthermore, most licensees were highly leveraged, forcing many to seek loan restructuring or bankruptcy relief when cash-flow projections consistently fell short.

In light of the changed landscape of the radio industry and the current economic climate, it is not surprising that the goals of localism and viewpoint diversity have come under increasing scrutiny. Today, regulators must endeavor to strike a balance between the economic interests of the radio industry and the important public-interest goals of localism and diversity. Congress, the Commission and the courts have all addressed the significance of diverse broadcast ownership and the importance of localism. Regulators, therefore, should continue to nurture these goals and attribute to them the appropriate priority in future regulatory actions.

Radio ownership rule changes

During 1992, declining revenues in the radio industry prompted the FCC to revise its ownership rules in order to stimulate greater efficiencies. In an attempt to address the changing economic prospects for the industry, the FCC relaxed national and local ownership limits. During the decision process, the FCC struggled concerns about localism and radio ownership diversity.

Since that decision, the industry has witnessed greater consolidation of ownership interests in radio stations among media conglomerates and group owners. Further consolidation in the ownership or joint operations will continue to reduce the number of separately owned voices that service the radio audience, which ultimately could decrease the diversity of program choices delivered to U.S. listeners.

The new radio ownership and time-brokerage rules promulgated by the Commission in August 1992 were intended to alleviate the economic plight of station owners hurt by the recession of the early 1990s. The 1992 National Association of Broadcasters (NAB) Financial Report highlights the negative revenues impact of the recession. Total revenues in 1991 were down 2.7 percent for FM stations, 6.6 percent for full-time AMs, and 10 percent for daytime AMs.

The new rules increased the national radio ownership limitations from 12 AM and 12 FM stations to 18 of each in 1992, rising to 20 and 20 by 1994. The new local rules permit a broadcaster to own up to four stations (two AM and two FM) within a large market (more than 15 stations) so long as the combination does not control more than 25 percent of the total audience. In smaller markets, a broadcaster can own up to three stations, if no more than two are in the same service (AM or FM), and if the combination does not control more than 50 percent of the market share. Under the new rules, a broadcaster who reaches the 18-station national limit (or the 20-station national limit as of 1994) can hold a noncontrolling interest in six (three AM and three FM) additional small-business or minority-controlled stations. The rules define minority-controlled as stations more than 50 percent owned by a minority group. Small businesses are defined as "an individual or business entity...[with] annual revenues of less than $500,000 and assets of less than $1,000,000." The prior rules provided that a minority broadcaster that reached the limit of 12 stations could own two additional stations.

The 18/18 national ownership limit is a scaled-down version of an earlier FCC proposal that the caps be increased to 30/30 with no incentive for minority ownership. Radio industry members and observers were divided over the propriety of such a rule, while members of

RADIO STATION EXPENDITURES, 1991

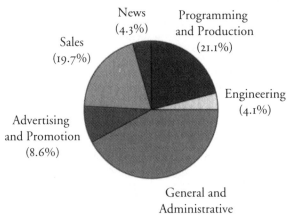

News
(4.3%)

Programming
and Production
(21.1%)

Sales
(19.7%)

Engineering
(4.1%)

Advertising
and Promotion
(8.6%)

General and
Administrative
(42.1%)

Source: National Association of Broadcasters, 1992

RADIO STATION INCOME SOURCES, 1991

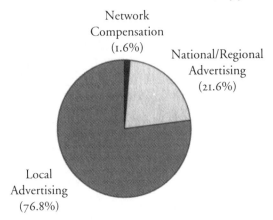

Network
Compensation
(1.6%)

National/Regional
Advertising
(21.6%)

Local
Advertising
(76.8%)

Source: National Association of Broadcasters, 1992

Congress expressed their opposition, threatening to freeze the limit at the level of 12 AM and 12 FM with one AM-FM combination permitted per local market.

The amendments to local ownership rules received great attention. Prior to the rule revision, a broadcaster was prohibited from owning two AM or two FM stations in the same principal city, although single AM/FM combinations were allowed. The cap was lifted to permit ownership of two AMs and two FMs in large markets and three stations in smaller markets, provided all three stations are not on one band. The 1992 radio rule revisions resulted in a rush of filings for the new station combinations—called local duopoly deals; 170 duopoly deals either have been announced or filed with the FCC since the new rules went into effect.

In lifting the cap, the Commission provided radio operators with an opportunity to own several stations in a market and enjoy joint ownership efficiencies such as consolidation of facilities, staffs, promotion and programming. Potential savings from such efficiencies allow station owners to compete more effectively in markets undergoing significant restructuring. At the same time, those radio broadcasters who are excluded from new duopoly deals face greater pressures to consolidate or to conduct joint ventures that reduce operating expenses. The only other alternative may be significant reductions of individual station operating costs.

The increased use of local marketing agreements (LMAs), or time-brokerage arrangements, also may contribute to future consolidation trends. With LMAs, a station owner sells "discrete blocks of time to a broker, who then supplies the programming to fill the time and sells the commercial spot announcements to support it." Generally stronger stations in a local market will undertake the advertising sales and possibly some of the programming of the other station. Although the healthier station conducts a great portion of the brokered station's operations, control of the brokered station is deemed to remain in the hands of the licensee. More than 158 LMAs have been established since 1990.

After considering whether LMAs should be regulated, the FCC concluded that limited restrictions on the practice were necessary. These restrictions include limiting control by another broadcast entity in the market of a brokered station's airtime to 15 percent a week, and a prohibition against duplicating more than 25 percent of a licensee's programming on another station in the same service (AM or FM). These limitations are designed to ensure that LMAs are not used to undermine ownership control and diversity in local markets.

New technologies and the multichannel world

In addition to the economic climate, emerging digital audio technologies also may influence the traditional public policy goals of localism and program diversity. Such audio technologies include digital audio broadcasting (DAB), which, in concept, will provide compact-disc-quality reception via satellite or in-band terrestrial transmissions to end users, and cable radio, which involves transmission of audio signals across coaxial cable.

Proponents of satellite DAB services generally have indicated a lack of interest in local programming, however, and provisions to accommodate viewpoint diversity, such as minority or small-business ownership incentives, also have not been addressed by either satellite or in-band DAB backers. The FCC is considering the applications of six parties who are interested in providing satellite DAB, and traditional broadcast interests have urged that regulatory safeguards be applied to DAB in order to protect localism.

Cable radio already is offered to approximately 2 million subscribers throughout the United States. Cable radio operators devote programming time to specific all-music or all-talk formats, with little emphasis on local news, weather or public affairs programming.

Development of these new digital radio services is part of a larger movement to integrate digital communications technologies into the broadcast industry. Digital technologies promise to change every aspect of the broadcast, cable and telecommunications industries. Today, radio broadcasters are under pressure to incur the costs and reap the benefits of the future digital world. Technological improvements in cable and broadcast television services—digital compression, high-definition television (HDTV) and interactive video and data services—force the industry to evaluate how it will compete in the multichannel world of the future. A byproduct of these new technologies will be the possibility of converting the television set into an interactive digital information tool, which would permit audiences to interact with a variety of entertainment, education or public affairs programs on demand. Such technologies on the horizon raise pointed questions for the radio industry. Radio operators will be required to make themselves attractive to audiences that become accustomed to a variety of interactive programming choices.

In addition to developments emerging from the FCC's 1992 radio ownership rule revisions and from potential of new digital radio services, last spring the Commission authorized the expansion of the AM band to 1605-1705 kHz. This decision could yield as many as 200 to 300 new AM stations nationwide. As an initial matter, the AM expanded band will be available only to existing broadcasters who can reduce signal interference by migrating from the existing AM band. No additional provisions for minority or female ownership of broadcast stations were incorporated in this decision.

The FCC has also been lobbied by certain broadcast interests to limit the number of licenses issued for FM stations in order to counterbalance the effects of 1980s deregulation. Additionally, some FCC commissioners have expressed support for broadcaster involvement in data and paging services through the use of the existing broadcast spectrum and new channels provided by digital technology. To provide data and paging services, broadcasters must receive FCC authorization to use their existing spectrum, the capacity of which can be expanded with digital technology, to accommodate the new services. Broadcasters might find that these new markets could be profitable supplements to their radio operations. Many broadcasters have already diversified their interests by entering markets such as newsletter publishing, television program production and on-line news services. If these rule modifications are made, both measures could help radio broadcasters compete with alternative audio, multichannel delivery systems, such as cable radio and DAB.

Traditional values: Localism and diversity

The FCC, with congressional and judicial support, has long placed priority on the issues of localism and viewpoint diversity as authorized in Section 307(b) of the Communications Act. Congress established the FCC in 1934 to serve and protect the "public convenience, interest or necessity" in licensing radio stations. The Commission has pursued that mandate of serving the public interest by requiring station owners to serve their local communities and participate in the station's operation. These requirements comprise the idea of localism, a basic notion that the best practicable service to the public is rendered by the broadcaster who maintains close ties with the community served and who provides programming that responds to issues affecting residents of that community. Such performance has historically been an important factor in license renewal. Broadcasters serving local interests have provided poignant examples of how radio stations serve critical roles during a community crisis—as exemplified by media involvement in the aftermath of riots in Los Angeles following the first Rodney King trial.

The FCC also has promoted the public interest by supporting the diversification of broadcast ownership. Since 1970, it has invoked multiple local and national ownership and cross-ownership rules, also adopting minority ownership policies in 1978 to encourage further breadth of viewpoints. The Commission traditionally has two types of diversity goals. One is to prevent excessive control over broadcasting by a few entities. As early as 1938, the FCC denied an applicant who already controlled another station in that city, even though he was the only party seeking the license. Since that time, policy has evolved. Due to technological developments and increased competition, the Commission has relaxed its rules in several areas. The 1992 radio ownership rules reflect greater emphasis on operating efficiencies rather than strict numerical caps. Despite these deregulatory trends, concern over ownership concentration and its impact on viewpoint diversity remains a major regulatory issue.

The second goal of diversity is to encourage minority and small-business ownership. The FCC has long held, and the Supreme Court has affirmed, that diverse ownership fosters diverse programming viewpoints. Prior to this decision, the Supreme Court in 1990 reviewed the constitutionality of the Commission's minority-ownership policies and recognized that broadcast diversity was an important governmental interest. The court found that broadcasting could be regulated in a manner which would provide listeners with the "widest possible dissemination of information from diverse and antagonistic sources."

Although most of the Commission's rules and policies relating to diversity date to the late 1970s and early 1980s, they remain necessary. Market statistics highlight the ongoing need for rules that promote minority and small-business ownership. The National Information and Technology Agency reported last November that minorities owned 3.6 percent of AM stations (177 of 4,969) and 2.1 percent of FMs (98 of the 4,723), clear indication of the continuing need for significant improvement in this area.

Future trends

New radio ownership rules are resulting in a consolidation of owner-ship and operations; the trade press keeps a daily count of duopoly and LMA deals. As the consolidation trend continues, it will become in-creasingly difficult to promote and protect the public-interest goals of localism and diversity.

The extent of the consolidation trend also will depend on the underly-ing health of the U.S. economy. Although the new ownership rules were predicated on the recessionary effects of a stagnant economy, this con-dition may change in the future. Indeed, recent forecasts predicted in-creasing revenues for owners, and reports on industry performance for the first quarter of 1993 showed improvement. If the economic condi-tions for the radio industry improve, regulatory pressure for further re-laxation of ownership is likely to ease. The Commission then will be able to focus more readily on preserving public interest concerns.

Continuing technological advances are inevitable. Although the in-terest in localism currently is served by radio broadcasters, it remains a possibility that new audio services competing for listeners could eclipse broadcasters in market share, resulting in a lost emphasis on localism. If digital technology advancements continue, the future is likely to present a multichannel world where consumers can access a plethora of pro-gramming and information through many nontraditional delivery sys-tems. The challenge for radio broadcasters will be to harness the technologies of the digital world in order to provide a variety of pro-grams, including interactive CD-ROM, high-tech computer-imaging techniques and high-speed broadcast systems that allow radio stations to deliver text, data and limited interactive services. Using the over-the-air broadcast medium to communicate in a two-way, interactive system would revolutionize the way Americans use radio.

Broadcasters will continue to play an important role in covering im-portant community issues and in providing a sounding board for local concerns. Consumers will continue to enjoy over-the-air radio program-ming. Radio's challenge will be to continue to serve local and diverse interests in the ways it already does, while remaining competitive with new and emerging services.

Andrew C. Barrett is a commissioner at the Federal Communications Commission. Byron F. Marchant, the commissioner's legal adviser, and Naomi Travers, a legal intern, assisted in preparing this article.

17

Riding Radio's Technological Wave

Richard V. Ducey

For the most part, the technological challenges facing the radio industry rattle not the competitive premise of an industry but rather its creative premise. Radio is an intensely personal medium, both in concept and in execution. In no other media business do competitors expend proportionately so much time, effort and money to so thoroughly research and strategize over the audience's psyche.

Arguably, the technology of radio could be viewed as an afterthought—it is programming, not technology, that draws listeners to the medium. Radio has not only survived but thrived through countless technological revolutions over the years. And, although its niche in the media market has evolved, its place among audiences and advertisers has remained remarkably stable. Radio is a local and personal medium, qualities that give it the resiliency it needs to ride the technology wave, past and future.

Unlike the video marketplace, most of new audio technologies have done comparatively little to erode radio's basic strongholds. Compact discs, digital cable radio and potentially new competition from satellite digital audio broadcasting (DAB) have all begun strafing runs at radio audiences' loyalty. Radio has answered with more local and personal service. AM talk shows have energized and involved the American public's newly rediscovered political voices. Children, like my 9-year-old daughter and her friends, are returning to the medium of their parents as formats like Radio AHHS make the radio fun and special for them.

Radio comes with the morning coffee, is dependable company to and from work, puts a little zip into the office environment and may ease the way to sleep at night. No one cares about how radio gets there—it's not

159

the technology but the content. We don't relate to radio as technology, but as a friend, as a source of information, entertainment and companionship. Given its variety and individuality, radio becomes an extension and counterpoint to our own personalities.

In this brief overview of the technological backdrop influencing the course of broadcast radio, I will concentrate on just a handful of topics: AM improvement, DAB and radio broadcast data systems. While there are other technologies that could profitably be addressed here, these are among the most important technological developments shaping radio's future.

AM improvement. Ever since it was introduced in this country some 70 years ago, AM radio has been undergoing technological changes. The Federal Communications Commission has supported a number of AM improvements lately, including AM interference protection, a plan for licensing stations on the expanded AM band and endorsing new industry AMAX (AM maximum) standards for enhanced AM reception. The AM improvement campaign is focused on two fronts—developing better AM receivers and decreasing the level of interference on the band. In practice, this boils down to improved equipment and fewer stations on the traditional AM band, along with more encouragement for AM stereo transmission.

The AMAX program was initiated by the National Association of Broadcasters (NAB) in conjunction with the Electronic Industries Association and its National Radio Systems Committee (NRSC). The AMAX logo can be displayed on receivers whose manufacturers have complied with five facets of AM improvement: an audio bandwidth of at least 50-7500 Hz, a wide/narrow bandwidth control (either automatic or manual), a noise-reducing circuit designed to help eliminate certain kinds of radio frequency noise, the capability to connect an external antenna, and the capability of receiving the expanded AM band (i.e., 1605-1705 kHz).

One of the reasons that AM receivers are not of higher quality is that radio receiver manufacturers see even an extra 50 cents as a significant expense. Motorola is developing a new noise-blanking integrated circuit chip. Major receiver manufacturers including both Japanese firms and companies like the Tandy Corporation and Thomson Consumer Electronics are interested in the Motorola chip as a cost-effective AM upgrade. The NAB worked with Denon to produce a "super" receiver incorporating all the AMAX specifications that was introduced to warm critical reception in audiophile publications.

AM stereo is a radio technology whose time has never come. Extensive market research sponsored by the NAB revealed that the dramatic flip-flop in listening patterns between AM and FM (from 75 percent AM listening to 75 percent FM listening in less than 15 years) was due not to superior FM technology alone, but also to FM's innovative and more attractive programming. Nonetheless, many believe that AM's monophonic limitations contributed significantly to the audience listening shift toward FM.

In 1992, Congress passed a law requiring the FCC to establish an AM stereo standard, something it refused to do in the early 1980s when such a standard would have made a bigger impact in the industry. While AM broadcasters will not be required to broadcast in stereo, coherence will be added to the marketplace by identifying a single stereo standard. The NAB's choice for the AM stereo standard is Motorola's C-Quam system. Although the perception is that AM radio means talk radio, 69 percent of AM stations broadcast music for at least part of the day; once the FCC selects an AM stereo standard, as Congress has now directed it to do, more stations may be encouraged into stereo upgrades, which will improve the sound quality of music on AM. This, in combination with competitive programming offerings, can only help AM.

To help clear up the clutter on the traditional AM band (which runs from 535 to 1605 kHz), the FCC is opening up 10 new AM channels (1605-1705 kHz) for development, initially by existing AM broadcasters willing to relocate from the lower band. Estimates are that up to 300 AM stations nationwide eventually can be accommodated on these new frequencies of the expanded band. Operators of daytime AM stations in cities of more than 100,000 people without full-time AM or FM stations will get preference, as will those proposing AM stereo operations. Radio manufacturers have been building receivers capable of receiving the extended AM band for years.

Digital Audio Broadcasting. One of the key technological trends driving all sectors of the telecommunications industry—not just radio—is digital technology. Digital audio services are now already offered by cable systems and are planned for both terrestrial and satellite services.

The advantage of DAB, of course, is much better sound quality on both AM and FM. DAB represents the first major technological breakthrough in terrestrial radio transmission in about 50 years. It is far superior to AM or even FM when it comes to no interference—CD-quality audio, lower power and maintenance costs and high-spectrum efficiency.

For broadcasters, the good news is that digital audio looks as if it can be offered within the same bands and even the same channels as existing AM and FM broadcasting. In 1993, the NRSC, a key industry group, voted to begin voluntary standard setting for in-band, on-channel DAB systems. Testing of competitors' systems (there will probably be five) for potential selection as the industry standard began in summer 1993.

This NRSC action is important for several reasons. First, as we learned with AM stereo, selection of a standard—whether by industry or government—is often critical to a technology's success. Second, by pursuing an in-band, on-channel option, the opportunity exists to reach the broadcast industry's goal of transition into digital audio without requiring additional spectrum while accommodating the existing AM and FM services. Both AM and FM digital audio broadcasting systems have been demonstrated.

Although prospects for terrestrial radio might seem solid, in truth, the first potentially significant competitor looms on the horizon—actually, somewhere above the horizon. The FCC has five applications for DAB satellite systems, which means that for the first time, radio faces a competitor capable of delivering over-the-air signals of DAB quality directly into homes, cars and other places where people listen to radio. This widely mobile reception capability strikes at the heart of one of radio's longtime competitive advantages.

Satellite DAB emerged in 1990, when Satellite CD Radio of Washington, D.C., filed the first application with the FCC; four others followed, and industry response is mixed. The industry is concerned about potential technical disruptions, particularly in the 7 GHz band, and with potential market dislocations with adverse consequences for the listening public.

The broadcast industry argues that this country already has a remarkably rich and diverse radio industry. Although the U.S. system of commercial radio is now emulated around the world, it has a finite economic base in which many stations are already losing money. To permit a large number of new satellite radio services to flood the market may undermine the remaining economic vitality that supports existing locally based radio services. But satellite DAB proponents counter by saying that most radio advertising is local, which would be unaffected by satellite services; further, they say, DAB could offer significant new choices, particularly to rural listeners.

A relatively new but modestly growing competitor is digital cable radio. Digital cable radio is typically a pay option to cable subscribers, and ranges in price from $10 to $13.50 per month for a mix of commercial-free digital audio programming. Since more than one-third of cable subscribers own CD players, they are accustomed to the benefits of digital audio sound.

Radio broadcast data systems. FM radio (and to a lesser extent, AM) has long made use of additional spectrum capacity to offer subsidiary services such as Muzak, stock quotes or paging. This capability is about to explode, offering new revenue streams to the industry and value-added services to the public. Radio broadcast data systems (RBDS)—basically a digital data stream transmitted through the 57 kHz subcarrier—has manufacturers eager to get into the business of RBDS radio receivers, and although it is largely an FM technology, the new standard established by the FCC in 1993 also accommodates AM.

Interestingly, format scanning—one of the features of RBDS that is most intriguing to radio receiver manufacturers—has not attracted much interest. Largely a European innovation, the technology was developed to permit listeners to follow the same programming while traveling cross-country by enabling their receivers to automatically scan and search out the nearest station playing their preferred service. While this may have some interest for U.S. listeners, given the vastly different competitive environment and listening habits, it is not clear that it will drive receiver sales to the extent manufacturers may expect.

Some of the specific features of RBDS systems are based on the use of transmitted data that can be displayed on screens in new radio receivers—station call letters or slogans, for example. Stations can also display up to 64 characters of text, such as song titles, artist names, weather updates, sports scores or sponsored information. Using other embedded data in the transmission, stations would identify their format for automatic scanning and selection by RBDS receivers. So listeners traveling through broadcast markets could tell their scanners to select preferred formats—country or classical or new wave—and to tune in to the preferred format station with the strongest signal, which would be useful in selecting between a parent station and a translator, for example. Emergency announcements could be sent over RBDS and a special trigger could even switch a radio from cassette or CD to radio (or even turn a radio on) in case of an emergency signal. Finally, RBDS would clearly support consumer services such as paging, though, because the capacity of the data stream is limited, at the expense of some other options.

Radio has endured despite threats from telephone, newspapers, television, cable, CD players, digital audio tape players and even its own dramatic explosion of stations serving the American public. Clearly, given all that cutthroat competition in the internecine struggle in the media family, there is still room for the oldest electronic survivor. The long-term lesson is this: Radio is a part of the American culture and continually reveals an unsinkable ability, if not to prosper, at least to maintain and grow. While radio may or may not be able to anticipate an "endless summer," it does have the basic ingredients for riding out yet another wave of technological innovation, just as it has done so often in the past.

Richard V. Ducey is senior vice president of the research and information group, the National Association of Broadcasters in Washington, D.C.

18

On the Business Side, an End to Radio Romance

Richard J. MacDonald

For most financial analysts, the days when the radio industry stood center stage have long passed. Few practitioners in the field have anything but oral history to generate even the vaguest images of radio's preeminence in the media field.

In the 1980s, the incentives to focus on radio were minimal. Although interest has reawakened of late, the improvement is narrow. Audio media are financially Lilliputian in scope, compared to the gargantuan visual media: television and film. In a world of scarce resources, devoting too much time to radio means nickels and dimes, relatively speaking. In the world of megamergers and acquisitions on Wall Street, the gross value of the average-sized AM radio station trade, for example, would be rejected as a fee too small to command the firm's resources.

Lack of interest among major Wall Street houses in the 1980s did not diminish trading in radio stations, however. For those great hunters pursuing media industry elephants, trading activity in the radio market became a kind of night sound that reached a furious hum toward the end of the decade. The number of radio stations changing owners annually rose from 614 in 1982—7 percent of all stations—to an astonishing 1,168 in 1986, about 13 percent of all radio properties. From 1982 to 1986, more than half of all commercial radio stations changed hands. Since 1987, the pace has dropped back to 1982 levels—600, about 6 percent of all stations, a year.

The same picture emerges more sharply focused in the dollar volume of stations traded. From 1982 to 1986, radio station sales rose from $602 million to $3.4 billion. From 1986 through 1989, the cumulative value of radio stations bought and sold equaled $9.1 billion, about 20 percent more than one year's total sales of advertising time. Since 1987, the value of radio station volume has also returned to 1982 levels on an absolute basis. Adjusted for inflation, the dollar value of traded stations may now be less than one-tenth of that traded in 1988.

Unlike newspapers or television, radio is a fiercely competitive business with little financial margin for error. But buyer errors were not minor—they were fundamental, based on unrealistic expectations of advertising growth and credit supply.

As it turned out, station asset values crashed after 1987, with the average station price nationwide dropping from a peak of $4.3 million in 1988 to $1.3 million in 1992. To overstate the case a little, a buyer who paid an average price for a radio station in 1988 and sold it for the average price in 1992 lost about 75 percent of his investment, assuming he didn't borrow to buy the station. (If he did, his bank also lost money.)

Two factors combined to destroy the value of radio stations in the 1980s. The first was a collapse of advertising spending, the second the collapse of credit.

The growth in billings for the average station began weakening in 1987 and turned negative in 1991. Part of the weakness was clearly due to a nationwide loss in confidence by consumers and businesses, which reached a nadir during the Gulf war. People stopped buying new cars, furniture and clothes—items typically advertised on radio. But underneath there lay a secular source of the slackness in demand as well—the impact on the radio industry of the "Walmart effect."

Sam Walton's chain of megastores, Walmart, held up as the supreme model for a new American competitiveness, often devastated retail competition in markets where they locate. And as local retailers struggle, their advertising budgets dry up.

"Walmart is a huge problem, especially in smaller markets," says Paul Fiddick, president of Heritage Media's radio group. "Walmart decimates the retail community when it comes in." Initially, Walmart uses radio to establish itself in a community but casts it aside once the competition is gone. The existing retail community "fades away and then is transformed and comes back in niches around the Walmart," Fiddick says. In the early days after a Walmart opening, the chain uses its great buying power in the local radio market to dominate and then eliminate the mom-and-pop competition. Once the original retail community is cleared, however, radio is less essential to the megastore and becomes a commodity supplier, which Walmart can squeeze as hard as any other of its vendors. Meanwhile, the "tent market" that forms in strip malls around the walls of Fortress Walmart needs less advertising and promotional support than before because the new vendors deal in specialties that don't compete with Walmart. Why advertise when shoppers flock to the "mother store" already and you can nab traffic coming and going?

In major markets, some operators claim that, if anything, the advent of Walmart causes retailers to buy their advertising more efficiently, although it's also true that in large markets, Walmart's challenges are greater—land is less abundant, labor is less malleable and the competition is better armed. In any case, some radio operators argue that stations benefit because cost control and efficiency become crucial under a Walmart assault. Radio is the least expensive and most targeted medium for retailers, a smart buy in competing against Walmart. But there's no indication in industry advertising numbers that radio has benefited anywhere from Walmart invasions in major markets, which acccount for the bulk of advertising spending. The Walmart effect is a net negative for radio.

Even apart from the unexpectedly sharp slowdown in revenues and cash flow in the last decade, radio was unattractive to bankers and investors alike during the liquidity crisis of the late '80s. One result was that credit for potential buyers of radio stations evaporated.

In an effort to prevent future S&L debacles, the federal government began stricter interpretations of its bank regulations. The most relevant and devastating to the media industry were the so-called highly leveraged transactions (HLT) rules. The HLT rules forced banks to categorize loans as highly leveraged (i.e. bad) if they exceeded a certain percentage of the hard assets of the borrowing company. Specifically excluded as tests of credit-worthiness were measures of financial health based on the notion of predictable cash flow in protected long-lived consumer franchises. A hard-asset test may have had relevance in the Industrial Revolution, when bricks and mortar and machines and equipment made up the real assets of the enterprise, but in an information society where assets are people, brand names and ideas, it is foolhardy.

For the radio station asset market, the consequences were brutal. Credit simply vanished. Banks stopped lending and, in an effort to comply with rules, sought to reduce their highly leveraged loans as a percentage of total portfolios. Radio lending was uniquely victimized in this process. As the bulk of outstanding HLT loans were enormous credits to companies like Time Warner, McCaw Cellular and others, banks could not call in such loans without jeopardizing their entire portfolios. But radio credits, tiny in comparison, could be called in without any fiscal repercussions (except, of course, to the radio industry).

The result was a flurry of bankruptcies in the radio industry.

So is there any hope for radio, economically speaking?

Such hope as exists ought to be measured soberly. Advertising spending rebounded in 1993, report national media companies, but that resurgence seems spotty. After the Clinton presidential victory, an initial surge of confidence swept consumers and advertisers alike, but that has waned and needs a further boost to support continued gains in advertising spending. Despite strong gains in the stock prices of radio companies, knowledgeable participants remain very cautious. "Equities [in radio] are up appreciably because investors are looking for strong gains in revenue and explosive cash flow growth from duopolies," observes Mike Connelly, an investment banker with Donaldson, Lufkin, Jenerette. It still isn't clear, however, who benefits from duopolies and what the benefits are.

One source of investor optimism was the federal response to crisis in the radio industry. When things got so bad that some 56 percent of all stations were losing money, by the middle of 1992, the government had responded in two ways: the HLT rules were rescinded, and the FCC expanded the number of licenses an individual operator could hold in any one market. The "one-to-a-market rule" was imposed in the 1930s to induce competition in network radio by breaking up the NBC Red and Blue radio networks. By the 1990s, however, the rule had outlived its usefulness by at least three decades. By allowing operators to create so-called duopolies, the FCC hoped to eliminate destructive competitive incentives and to improve the financial viability of radio properties.

From an operator's perspective, investing in a second station in the market brings competitive peace of mind and new opportunities to save money. Many hope there will be new revenue opportunities as well. But whether duopolies can generate new advertising is not at all clear. Herb McCord's Granum Communications has recently closed on a duopoly transaction in Boston. For McCord, Boston is a laboratory. "We don't really know what to expect," he says. His two stations will function as a hybrid, each with separate programming and sales staff, but a single general manager, business manager and operations budget. Another with a duopoly in the Boston market, Infinity Broadcasting, runs its stations almost as if they were competing, maintaining separate locations and formats. But another, Greater Media, operates its dual stations as a combined operation with the same signal and a single staff in one location.

But McCord and others worry that revenues will decline for combined stations, which is why he's hedging his bets in Boston. He thinks that advertisers will be resistant to stations pursuing tougher negotiating positions for duopolies. "You're dealing with people (advertisers) who have had their way a long time," he said. As one industry banker put it, "Two dogs still equals two dogs."

Even so, most seem confident that merging stations will mean cost savings and improvements in cash flow, profits and viability. Bringing together two stations under one management allows the operator to eliminate half the administrative overhead. In the Boston case, both the Granum and the Greater Media stations foresee cost savings. But Boston is unusual because it is a major market with three duopoly transactions in the works. For McCord, the cost savings for his stations are helpful but not crucial. For stations in smaller markets, on the other hand, savings from a duopoly could amount to $500,000 a year, or the difference between red ink and black.

Who gets the black ink and who gets stuck with the red has become an obstacle to completing duopoly deals, however. If a profitable station is trying to buy a weaker one, then the buyer naturally expects to benefit from the added value created by merging the two. But sellers argue that the additional value results only from *combining* the stations, and so hold out for better selling prices. Sellers whose stations are at least breaking even have little to lose in holding out for more money from the sale of the station, although stations that are losing money may be lucky to get "stick value" in the sale—the value of a fully licensed and equipped but dormant station.

Another key action by the government was to improve the flow of credit by eliminating the HLT designation, which prevented banks from lending to stations with high debt-to-asset ratios. Without bank finance, station buyers must put up all their own money, which substantially reduces the pool of the buyers and theoretically limits the returns to radio investments. But in reality, no credit means no buyers.

There is some credit available for radio deals today. Bankers like the simplicity of radio. But operators for whom the HLT period meant no credit now are skeptical. Bank lending to radio is an abominable snowman: "There have been sightings, I'm told, but no real encounters with the beast," one operator said. Banks may be willing to look at duopolies, he added, but there doesn't seem to be any market for loans to nonmonopoly stations.

In fairness, many bankers got burned in the late 1980s by bad loans to radio. As a result, they're cautious and much more focused on fundamentals. "Management is the most important thing we look at," says Deborah Rasin, senior vice president at Bank of New York, which stayed in communications through the HLT period. "You can have a great [station] in a great market and still lose money. If a competitor attacks you with a format change, you've got to have a management that knows what to do, how to handle it."

A second important consideration for banks is diversity within their own communications portfolio. "You can have a competitor go crazy overnight and launch a format change that you have to respond to," Rasin said. "You have to have those other stations to get cash flow from." Which is the principal attraction of duopoly for bankers—stability. "What that means is that a station can protect its flanks from chipping away by competitors," she said. "Changing formats can be an 18-month investment and very expensive to your cash flow."

In making loans to radio operators, bankers will consider cost savings from duopolies in calculating credit-worthiness but not potential revenue gains. "There are some cost savings in duopolies that you can give credit for," Rasin said, "but we still want no more than five times debt to cash flow. Debt is still debt if something goes wrong, something bankers forgot in the late '80s." This means that buyers must put up the difference if the debt-to-assets ratio is greater than 5-to-1. For a station with a sale price seven times its cash flow, for example, the bank will lend five times the cash flow, and the buyer must put up the rest—two times the cash flow.

Such transactions typically occur between people who are professional radio managers seeking control over the radio property; for them, their destiny rests in their own hands. So industry players were astonished at the premiums paid by stock market players, investors with no operating control over the investment. As Paul Fiddick says, "The Evergreens and the Infinities are trading at nine and 10 times operating cash flow in the public market. For someone in the business that does not make any sense—even if you liquidated the whole company and sold every asset, you still wouldn't get your equity back. It's crazy."

Crazy, maybe, but one of the most hopeful financial signs for radio is that raising equity is easier than raising bank debt. Recently, Infinity, Evergreen and Saga Communications all raised new equity from public investors and have already rewarded them with solid returns. "People think there is a coming explosion in cash flow," says investment banker Mike Connelly. Investors read *any* significant increase in the public share price as Delphic, of course, but this is a hopeful sign. "The market is telling us something," he says. It is a bright day when the inherent optimism of the equity market supplants the dreary calculus of credit analysis, balancing the banker's green eyeshade myopia with the vision (albeit often naive) of the equity player and entrepreneur.

The results of these economic trends and the financial markets' response to regulatory changes already are becoming clear. Elimination of HLT and the duopoly rules already are driving the radio industry to consolidation. Inevitably, market forces will ensure that radio groups will become larger and more corporate. In the end the stand-alone station in a small market with a singular personality, a unique voice, a quirky and even risky format will be absorbed, forgotten or left to public funding.

Just as inevitable will be changes in the content of radio. Increasingly, the sensible interests (not especially greedy, even) of bankers and group owners will dominate what we hear on the airwaves, streamlining it as an ever more efficient advertising vehicle and cash-flow producer. For stations pursuing their own notions of what people want to hear, their interests have been left untended. For many of these, one result of market forces on the radio industry may be the end of an old romance between the solitary listener and a station call sign that once evoked some lost place or time.

Richard J. MacDonald, a 1992–93 fellow at The Freedom Forum Media Studies Center, is a media analyst and investment banker with FirstBoston in New York.

19

Public Radio—Americans Want More

Anna Kosof

In 1967, Congress authorized funds to create an agency to foster the growth and development of public broadcasting. The Corporation for Public Broadcasting (CPB) had important ramifications for television, but its impact on the radio industry was even greater. This historic legislation extended radio's voice to thousands of Americans in hundreds of communities, expanding public radio availability to 86 percent of the U.S. population.

Public radio had been around since 1949, when the Pacifica Foundation started KPFA in Berkeley, Calif.—this country's first station run by a nonprofit community group. Based on the premise that commercial-free radio and free speech were important, and coming from the left of U.S. mainstream ideology, Pacifica thrived, soon acquiring four more stations in major markets, including New York and Washington, D.C., and developing an award-winning, hour-long alternative news format. Besides nurturing creative talent, Pacifica also created the means for independent producers to experiment and learn their craft—it was a training ground to press the limits of public radio.

The creation of National Public Radio (NPR) in 1970 established an unprecedented national identity, sound and mission for public broadcasting. Initially viewed as an alternative in the radio world, a voice for the unserved public through direct, unrestricted CPB funding, the mission, character and purpose of noncommercial radio have evolved over the past two decades clearly in response to commercial broadcasting.

The CPB legislation intended that public radio serve an audience that commercial radio saw as unviable or otherwise undesirable. In early

1993, there were 11,338 on-air radio stations in this country, about 86 percent commercial—9,743 were commercial AMs and FMs, and 1,592 noncommercial or public stations. Among other things, public broadcasting has shown that audiences do exist for program formats abandoned by commercial radio as nonviable. In music, for example, jazz and classical represent just 0.6 percent of commercial programming, reports *M Street Journal*, an industry newsletter; about half of 1 percent (46) play classical music and about the same number are committed to jazz. By contrast, of the 1,592 noncommercial stations in the United States, 275 (17.2 percent) are classical and 72 (about 4.5 percent) program jazz exclusively.

The most basic goals for selling any product are a clearly defined market, knowledge of the consuming audience, an understanding of audience needs and creation of a unique product (or, in this case, format) designed to meet those needs. Commercial radio could not have done a better job of defining the market for noncommercial radio. Since the mission for public radio is to serve an underserved audience and to provide alternatives, public radio needed simply to target those left behind by commercial stations.

Recent regulatory trends may further define the market for public radio. Although changes in FCC rules that will permit single owners to operate up to four radio stations in a given market surely will benefit large broadcast conglomerates, public radio also will gain as commercial radio scrambles for the most lucrative niches, abandoning more audience segments as unviable. Some industry observers think the feeding frenzy may result in a drop of as many as 25 percent in the number of stations as large commercial companies purchase and consolidate stations, including (especially) the most idiosyncratic small-scale, mom-and-pop operations. Obviously, commercial broadcasters consider only the most financially rewarding formats. Thus, formats such as classical music or jazz, or 90-minute news/public affairs programs like "All Things Considered" or "Monitor Radio," probably won't interest buyers in quest of the prime demographic. Thus, as commercial and noncommercial broadcasters find themselves farther apart and serving very different needs, a fertile ground is created for the growth of public radio.

In many ways, public broadcasting is an oddity in America. Although funded by dues, members and nonmembers get the same product regardless of whether they pay or not. In a consumption-oriented culture, listener-supported radio is a peculiar concept. Only one in 10 public radio listeners actually pays to support the local station—the highest percentage is in Vermont, where 12 percent of listeners ante up during pledge drives. Even so, membership levels increased nationwide during the 1980s to more than 1,300,000. For what it's worth, that's more members than the National Rifle Association. Government commitment to the concept of public broadcasting is reflected in the relative levels of support in the United States, United Kingdom and Canada: annual funding for all public broadcasting in this country amounts to $1.06 per person, $38.15 for Britain's BBC and $32.15 for Canada's CBC.

Still, public broadcasting in the United States has found its definition over the past 20 years. In the mid-1970s, Pacifica on-air personalities begged for airtime, not for salary but for the creative freedom to produce programs catering to a different lifestyle, out of the Nixon-Ford-Carter post-Vietnam mainstream. Unconcerned with underwriting or audience size, and still in the process of developing member support, Pacifica's internal debates concerned the impact of accepting federal funds from the CPB. The fear was that any external funding would jeopardize Pacifica's mission. Ironically, it was during its leanest years, in the 1960s, that Pacifica made what may have been its greatest impact, with in-depth programs on the Vietnam War and alternative programming for voices that could be heard nowhere else.

When NPR was formed in 1970, many of Pacifica's best and brightest went there, and the Pacifica legacy expanded. Chris Koch, who reported nightly for Pacifica from Hanoi, became the executive producer of "All Things Considered." Margot Adler, a veteran Pacifica talk and news producer, became NPR's New York bureau chief. Marty Goldensohn, another Pacifica graduate, is New York bureau chief of American Public Radio's "Marketplace." For these and many others, Pacifica was a training camp for some of the most highly regarded reporters in public radio of the 1990s.

Many who joined NPR developed programs that reached beyond the fringe audiences, refining what really has become the personality of public radio. As the characters of commercial radio and public radio have become more defined, NPR and APR, while maintaining their identity as alternatives to commercial fare and champions of the free-speech audiences that flocked to Pacifica in the 1960s and 1970s, are no longer the radical fringe. Alternatives to endless commercials laced with re-

peated top-40 hits, public radio stations have developed their own identities, whether through classical music, R&B or evening jazz formats, or
through the in-depth public-affairs programs such as "All Things Considered" that have become the NPR hallmark. This kind of programming and the baby boomers who have embraced it have made possible
public radio's coming of age in the 1990s, not just with a better defined
character but a more sophisticated sound.

New challenges to public radio come from within the industry and
from the new technology; both have serious consequences. Having created a system that programs for a largely white and affluent audience,
public radio needs new models as society recognizes its own ethnic evolution. For example, WBGO-FM, a minority-operated station in Newark, N.J., with a majority African-American audience, has developed
jazz and blues as its programming mission—being a catalyst to bring
people together through a common love for the music. Other stations do
the same. Radio station KILI, located on the Pine Ridge Reservation in
South Dakota, is the bedrock of the Lakota Native American community. It is the voice of a community where phones are scarce and the
listeners turn to KILI for essentials of survival, whether blankets on a
cold night or community news. Santa Monica's KCRW integrates NPR
programming with locally produced programs, offering an alternative
to the dreadful wasteland of commercial middle-of-the-road.

These examples (and many more) offer a glimpse at how the nature
of public broadcasting has evolved. "Traditional conceptions of the mission and the role of a local public radio station are changing," reports
the Station Resources Group (SRG), public radio's most important think
tank. "These changes are driven by powerful shifts in communications
technology, new priorities for public-sector funding, potent socioeconomic developments and the ambitions of the stations themselves." The
most pressing goals for public radio stations, the SRG says, may not be
so different from those of commercial radio: "hard-nosed scrutiny of
current operations and programming, a realignment of investments and
services and the creation of new, more ambitious development goals."

The challenge is the same as it has been. Public radio today will have
to be revisited and reexamined in order for the next generation of public
radio to survive and flourish. But some of the challenges and needs remain the same as when Pacifica started KPFA in 1949. In the vast and
rapidly growing cultural diversity of this country, there still exists an

increasingly large underserved niche that public radio must fill. Representation of local issues will ensure its survival and enlarge its niche in the communications field. As more commercial stations begin to operate from corporate headquarters and as more small operators are forced out, even fewer local voices will be represented. This will create an even greater need for public radio and its mission to provide an alternative, community-based voice.

Paradoxically, technological development may be a downside to the opportunities of economic consolidation of the commercial radio market. While market forces may offer new niches for public radio to reach underserved or abandoned audiences, new technologies may step in between those audiences and local stations. Unlike its partner, public television, radio has not yet come to the next challenge that cable television presents, but the dawn is not far off. Hundreds of new channels soon may emerge through digital satellite transmissions, duplicating and supplanting existing stations. Today, public radio has no major competition in most markets. New technology and changing demographics will require that public radio—as well as commercial broadcasting—think fast and hard about the kind of programming that it has presented and fine-tuned over the last two decades, and what it will offer in the future.

Public radio's most important asset is its localism and the special relationship listeners develop with programs and those on the air. That special relationship is the lifeblood of the station. Listeners who talk to on-air personalities by their first names—Bob, Cokie, Nina, Neil, Susan, Noah, Garrison, Linda—see public broadcasting as *theirs*, part of their family or circle of close friends. These are the committed members, the most important element in the survival and growth of public radio.

In these times of economic recession and corporate, academic and governmental downsizing, public stations must frantically seek a higher percentage of revenues from membership. In so doing, they must revisit their own missions and examine how to maintain the programming quality that listeners expect. In some ways, the economic climate has turned back the clock on public radio, to a time of much greater reliance on public support. While public broadcasting has became more commercialized over the years, some with roots in the early revolutionary mission of public radio are less than perturbed over threats to its underwriting and sponsorships. In embracing commercialism, some say, public radio may have lost its mission and soul. Steve Post, a veteran public radio broadcaster and host of WNYC's popular weekday morning classical music show, questions whether classical music or jazz is really public radio's main mission. Enhanced underwriting makes public radio sound increasingly commercial, he and others argue. If membership is the key to public radio's survival, it's past time for a return to that old sense of mission and public connection. The niche may exist within the increasingly culturally and ethnically diverse society. The key, as always, may be as simple as watching for audiences the commercial stations don't find economically attractive. Beyond the tote bag, coffee mug and program guide, people want more from radio than top 40, Limbaugh, the same news every 22 minutes and endless ads. That's where America—where public radio—lives.

Anna Kosof is a longtime public radio professional and communications consultant based in Newark, N.J.

20

Growing NPR

William E. Buzenberg

From obscure infancy some two decades ago, National Public Radio (NPR) has grown into something approaching celebrity. In the early 1970s, few would have ventured to say this broadcasting blip would survive, much less flourish and begin to set standards for quality in American broadcasting. NPR's success can be attributed to its own strengths and sense of mission, cutbacks and loss of direction elsewhere in the commercial marketplace, and a lot of luck.

It was lucky, for example, that 50 years ago "educational" radio was tucked safely out of the way on what was then thought to be the obscure end of the now-dominant FM dial. It was lucky that the 1968 federal legislation that created public television happened to include, almost as an afterthought, funding to start public radio. And it was lucky that a man from Buffalo, N.Y., named Bill Siemering knew what he was doing 22 years ago when he conceived an improbable 90-minute evening news magazine called "All Things Considered." Named *Washington* (now *American*) *Journalism Review*'s Best in the Business for years, the flagship "ATC" became the first NPR program inducted into the Radio Hall of Fame in November 1993.

For years considered insignificant, public radio can no longer be ignored as an upstart by bigger and better-financed commercial radio broadcasters. The size of NPR's growing and dedicated audience, as well as the kind of people who listen, clearly challenge old assumptions that public radio was just for "zither concert" types and well-heeled classical music buffs. From about 4 million listeners a week in 1983, the national NPR News audience has climbed to 10 million people who tune in to almost 500 NPR member stations nationwide. Every week, about 7 percent of Americans over age 12 listen to public radio, and in some cities, NPR stations now dominate—WBUR in Boston and KQED in San Francisco, as the best examples, rank at the top in their markets.

A recent Simmons study finds that NPR listeners are concentrated in the coveted 24-to-54 age group. They are well educated—more than half of NPR listeners have attended or graduated from college, well above the national average. Most live in households with annual incomes above $30,000, also more than the norm, and one of every three works in a professional or managerial capacity, twice the U.S. average. The NPR audience is influential in other ways. It is more involved in public activities, more apt to give to charities, and more apt to vote—70 percent compared to 59 percent of American adults. And they aren't all left-wing granola eaters, as the stereotype suggests: One-third of NPR listeners describe themselves as politically conservative; 25 percent say they are middle-of-the-road, and 29 percent consider themselves liberal.

Over the last 20 years, what has attracted listeners to public radio has changed considerably. At first considered a marginal "alternative" news source, NPR News produced just one 90-minute program each weekday, broadcast by fewer than 100 stations. Feature-driven with little in the way of breaking news, those early programs relied more on imagination than on reporters. The old joke was that we covered stories three days late and called it analysis.

Since then, NPR News has grown into a primary news source, offering 13 hours of news programming every day, seven days a week, including the national afternoon call-in program, "Talk of the Nation." In October 1993, NPR added newscasts around the clock; indeed, we may soon be able to provide a 24-hour news stream, as we did during peak news periods such as the Persian Gulf war.

The challenge of such growth has been to maintain NPR's commitment to quality. Bill Siemering set the standard for high quality when he launched "ATC" in 1971, demanding adherence to fundamentals that have remained at the core of NPR's appeal and its distinctive brand of radio journalism. NPR programs are valued not just because they are uninterrupted by commercial pitches, but because they use to the fullest what the medium of radio can offer. Siemering insisted on four basic elements: crisp, clear, memorable writing; imaginative sound production; authentic voices of people from outside the studio; and a conversational, accessible style. Add to that depth of analysis, careful, accurate editing, smart and sometimes courageous reporting, plus plenty of opportunity for what radio does best—imagination—and you have the NPR recipe. The NPR trademark combines seriousness of purpose with an appetite for curiosity, satire, whimsy and a willingness to laugh at ourselves (and others).

Indeed, NPR is not above making fun of radio itself, with a satirical spin of the radio dial. On April Fools Day, for example, no NPR broadcast has been complete without highly polished and highly fictitious reports on talking salmon, pickle ranching, compost salads, Wisconsin's fondue lakes or political upheaval in Trashkanistan. Also popular are listener contests (without trips or prizes). The best of these may have been a contest in early 1993 to help name the new offerings on the futuristic 500-channel cable TV systems. Contributions included "Span-Scam," the canned meat channel, and "Span-Span," the bridge-building channel.

But more than whimsy, NPR helps provide away to make sense of the world. Listeners often say National Public Radio helps them talk about issues, topics and ideas of the day—"Did you hear on NPR that…?" In effect, NPR listeners represent a community,whether they live in Missoula, Montana, or New York or Tulsa, linked by interests instead of geography, people who use the network as a mainstream listening post in a wide range of ongoing national debates.

Despite funding cutbacks by states and universities that support NPR stations, public radio budgets have been relatively stable, largely because of increases in audience and underwriter attention. Federal funding through the Corporation for Public Broadcasting (CPB) represents just 16 percent of station budgets, so while federal support is a significant factor, listener contributions and corporate underwriting have become even more important.

This cobbled-together funding structure results in an investment in news coverage that will approach $17 million in 1994, supporting about 50 NPR reporters and a team of program hosts, newscasters, editors and producers. With 12 full-time reporters overseas, NPR has a significant foreign news staff that rivals many other U.S. news organizations. NPR correspondents now report important stories from Sarajevo to Mexico

City, from Mogadishu to Moscow to Tokyo. Member stations have also been beefing up their own local news coverage. The 78 stations that make up the Public Radio News Directors group employ 177 full-time and 150 part-time reporters, helping public radio cover the nation in partnership with NPR. And NPR employs one of the most ethnically and racially diverse staffs in journalism—more than one-quarter minority and 52 percent female, figures that match national demographics. I know of no other U.S. news organization—mainstream or otherwise—that can match those numbers.

While public radio news has slowly but steadily grown, many commercial stations—radio and television alike—have been forced to cut back their news operations. In fact, over the past 10 years, about 4,000 commercial radio news jobs have been eliminated nationwide, reports the Radio-Television News Directors Foundation; except for cable, TV news also has been cutting back. In some cases, local talk shows or syndicated talk programs like Rush Limbaugh's and Larry King's have taken the place of more expensive news programs. The result, says *American Journalism Review*, is that talk radio with its mix of opinion and entertainment is crowding out serious radio news. (One former news director says his managers "wanted to hear more news about Jay Leno and less about the terrorist who bombed the World Trade Center.")

The trend in commercial broadcasting toward "infotainment" (or "Hollywoodization," as a gloomy Dan Rather put it recently), with shorter sound bites, more glitz and less depth, gives a boost to public radio's approach of focusing on context, background and, above all, providing understanding. In this environment, the advantage of radio as a medium of ideas, with the potential to develop solutions, is gaining currency. NPR senior news analyst Daniel Schorr has little patience for the trends in television, his former medium. "Television, by celebrating violence, promotes violence," he lamented recently. "By rewarding terrorism, it encourages terrorism. By trivializing great issues, it buries great issues. By blurring the lines between fantasy and reality, it crowds out reality." In the faces of this trend, the value of good public-affairs radio is growing.

With listener success, competition and imitation has come to public radio. American Public Radio (now known as Public Radio International) now distributes news programming—such as "Marketplace," funded largely by General Electric, or Monitor Radio, from the Christian Science Church—to many of the same public stations that buy NPR programs. A Baltimore radio executive is planning another competing public radio news network, to be called "Citizen's Public Radio." The Cable News Network (CNN) is selling its own radio news service to public stations, and Canada's CBC and the United Kingdom's BBC World Service provide additional international programming. As public radio's news audience has grown, so has the importance of those listeners to various providers.

Besides attracting competitors, NPR's success and increasingly high profile have also contributed to growing political pressure from Congress and the Corporation for Public Broadcasting. Originally established as a "heat shield" between the government and broadcasters to protect free expression from political pressures, the CPB has increasingly felt itself caught between a hands-off approach and an urge to stick a finger in the pie. As long as relatively few were listening, the politicians left public broadcasting largely alone. Now, however, under the guise of legislation requiring "objectivity and balance," there is a danger that the CPB could attempt to insert itself more directly in programming decisions. Certainly, no one objects to goals of "objectivity and balance," but in the American system, programming decisions are made by journalists, not by government-administered guidelines. For its part, consistent with tenets of the U.S. press, NPR maintains its insistence on complete independence.

NPR News programs deal with an enormous range and number of issues, including both those that are the most controversial and central to the day's national debate, and those that generally can count on much more cursory treatment in other media. Although we have plenty of critics, NPR includes a wider range of viewpoints and a far greater array of voices than almost any other broadcasting source, in keeping with NPR's mandate to expand the spectrum of news and opinion. Over the years, NPR has focused consistent attention on the journalistic standards and the professional quality of its work, balancing many points of view and striving to provide scrupulously fair treatment to the many sides of any issue.

One additional reason, among many, that it is important for public radio to maintain its independence from government—and thus its credibility as a respected American news source—is that the network has just entered the global broadcasting arena. In October 1993, NPR began providing programming directly to Europe on the World Radio Network (WRN) via the Astra satellite. So, in Helsinki, for example, Finnish citizens and foreign travelers now can tune in to programs such as "Morning Edition" and "Talk of the Nation," just like NPR listeners in Toledo and Tucson.

For some, it's the sound of home. "Hallo!" one listener faxed to the NPR newsroom from Europe. "Just heard your voice over the World Radio Network. Greetings from Berlin." Said another from the Netherlands, "I'm glad to hear 'All Things Considered' up on WRN. At last!" And a third: "Hi from the Grand Duchy (Luxembourg). We are listening now via WRN on Astra."

With continued national and international news reporting of high quality and around-the-clock programming that has achieved the credibility of the BBC, NPR may well emerge as a distinct voice of America for a global as well as a domestic audience. Not a bad legacy for an idea dismissed as "far out" more than 20 years ago.

William Buzenberg is vice president for news and information at National Public Radio in Washington, D.C.

21

Monopoly to Marketplace—Competition Comes to Public Radio

Stephen L. Salyer

When most people think of public radio, it's *National* Public Radio—NPR—that comes to mind. For most, "public radio" means both the local station they listen to and the programming they hear. Until recently, only industry insiders or very attentive listeners could distinguish between NPR and APR—American Public Radio—much less identify what programs each supplies.

Yet, as the Minneapolis-based *American* Public Radio (which became Public Radio International in July 1994) celebrated its 10th anniversary in 1993, APR surpassed NPR in its number of affiliated stations, distributed more hours of programming each week and accounted for a growing share of public radio station schedules and audience. How this has happened and what it has meant for public radio are parts of a story worth considering as the demands on limited public resources for broadcasting intensify and as policy-makers question whether competition might improve public services.

The APR story began in 1981 when public broadcasting started using a satellite to deliver programs from producers to affiliates. Previously, program producers had had only two options for reaching a national audience—shipping individual tapes directly to stations across the country or shipping them to NPR in Washington, D.C., which distributed the programs over phone lines. Both methods were slow, virtually ruling out the production of news or timebound material except by NPR. The use of Bell System long lines was efficient for less timely programming, but NPR's approval was required for a program to go out.

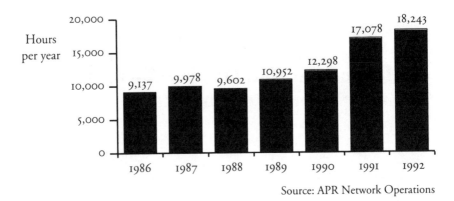

APR PROGRAM HOURS DISTRIBUTED

Source: APR Network Operations

Having both the largest producer and the only efficient distributor under one roof with the capability of sending out only one program at a time resulted in a built-in conflict between NPR and the many producers who aspired to have their programs heard nationally. Although many locally produced programs were of insufficient quality or interest to warrant national distribution, by the early 1980s a number of public radio's leading stations had begun to feel that NPR's decisions on what to distribute reflected too narrow a view of audience interests and underestimated the quality of station and independent production. A classic case involved a request by Minnesota Public Radio to distribute Garrison Keillor's "A Prairie Home Companion," then a local offering, as part of NPR's national program service. The request was denied, apparently because the program's appeal was deemed too narrow and its production values too low for national consumption.

The advent of satellite distribution meant programs could be uplinked to the satellite from multiple locations across the nation and that stations could receive up to 12 national offerings simultaneously. This opportunity was not lost on the most prolific of the nation's public radio station producers, five of which decided in 1982 to form American Public Radio Associates as a second national program service. Initially operated as a subsidiary of Minnesota Public Radio, the group dropped "Associates" from the name in 1983 and incorporated APR as a fully independent organization.

From the beginning, it was clear that APR represented more than just another program stream. It was privately operated with an independent board of directors, not "owned" by member stations or governed by an elected board of station managers like NPR and PBS. APR charged stations affiliation fees based not on the size of their budget, as did NPR, but on the size of their market or potential audience. Further, APR offered programs *à la carte*, while NPR offered stations its entire program service for a single price. And, in markets with more than one public radio station, APR offered programs on an exclusive basis, permitting enterprising stations the opportunity to establish a franchise and earn back the fees they were charged through increased listener contributions and local underwriting. In short, APR embraced principles of competition that were at that time foreign to public radio, functioned more like a commercial business than a membership organization and promoted the virtues of a program marketplace in which stations could select and purchase only those programs that met their local needs.

Not everyone in public radio welcomed such innovations. For station managers accustomed to paying one price for a large bundle of services, APR's pattern of offering programs with small or no initial fees, followed by a rapid price increase to market levels, left them feeling exploited and angry. For those accustomed to a vote on the annual NPR budget and at least some sense of participation in setting the network's direction, APR's method of setting priorities seemed mysterious and undemocratic. For those raised in a public radio system dependent largely on government support (especially those stations licensed to colleges or school boards), the fear was ever present that APR would siphon away support essential to the major NPR news programs.

Despite such concerns, APR rapidly gained affiliates, aided in part by unexpected difficulties at NPR. In 1983, NPR almost collapsed, largely the result of ill-fated commercial investments intended to replace cutbacks in federal support proposed by the Reagan administration. In the wake of a deficit that would have spelled bankruptcy for a commercial entity, NPR was forced to concentrate on saving its two major news magazines, "Morning Edition" and "All Things Considered," and all but abandoned cultural programming. APR filled the gap with high-quality

APR AFFILIATES

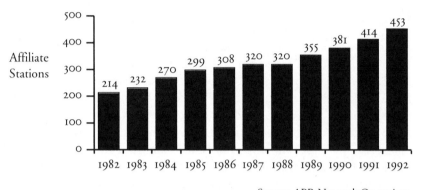

Source: APR Network Operations

classical music, comedy and variety programs, and its affiliation and program usage continued to climb. By the time Garrison Keillor made the cover of *Time* magazine in 1985, APR had established itself as public radio's leader in cultural programming, distributing almost 200 hours of programming each week.

NPR's financial difficulties—and extraordinary subventions required by its member stations and by the Corporation for Public Broadcasting to rescue the network—convinced many that more fundamental reforms were needed in public radio. Gradually, a consensus emerged in the industry that the best way to ensure sound national institutions was to make them more accountable to the stations—i.e., to the organizations licensed to serve the public interest and most directly accountable to listeners. In 1985, the CPB implemented a plan whereby NPR would no longer receive a significant portion of the federal appropriation for radio; rather, individual stations would receive the lion's share of resources and would then purchase programs and services they needed. (Congress subsequently required that the stations use a portion of federal funds to buy national programs, a requirement that continues to this day, and the CPB set up a modest Radio Program Fund to support development of new programs.) Over a remarkably short time,

APR's advocacy of a program marketplace had moved from the radical fringe into the mainstream.

Even after funds began flowing directly to stations, however, NPR resisted changing its policy of offering programs in bundles for a single price. That was understandable—NPR's two "must have" newsmagazines sustained other programs that never could have survived on their own. At one point, APR threatened to sue under the Sherman Antitrust Act if NPR failed to unbundle programming, and the network gradually yielded, at least in part, although NPR still offers morning and afternoon news and a single cultural package. APR continues to sell most major programs separately.

From its inception, APR also took a very different approach to program production than NPR, in large part to avoid the conflict between the role of program distributor and that of producer. NPR historically has produced many of its best known programs in-house, utilizing staff and studios paid for by member dues. APR has shunned the producer's role, choosing instead to invest in the development of new programs by leading stations and independent producers and in acquiring the best finished shows.

While this approach gives APR the flexibility to answer diverse station and listener needs, it initially limited its news capabilities. By definition, news and current affairs reporting is a costly business, as the commercial television networks have come to realize. NPR had benefited from 15 years of federal investment, in the tens of millions of dollars, by the time APR was formed.

While APR's mission embraced both news and cultural programming from the outset, the high cost of creating the necessary news infrastructure required a strategy different from NPR's. Relationships with the BBC World Service, then available to listeners only on short wave, and with the Canadian Broadcasting Service (CBC) solved some of those problems. These organizations offered APR the highest caliber news programming and gave listeners access to international perspectives not available elsewhere on the dial.

In addition, APR looked for niches unserved by NPR. One such opening was business and economics reporting, and APR sought alliances with other entities able to mount such programs. First, a radio version of the cable television program "Business Times" was distributed, with stations paying a portion of the cost. When the cable venture collapsed, however, a ground-breaking agreement was reached with CBS Radio to produce "Business Update," a program that offered CBS correspondents an opportunity missing in their own organization to do in-depth reporting. Although the program was a credible daily report, it failed to attract an underwriter and suffered from what many stations described as "an incompatible sound with NPR news," which typically led into the broadcast.

From these experiences, APR concluded that to be a player in domestic news, it would need greater production capacity at one or more places within public radio. The result was APR's largest single program investment—$500,000—to help establish a West Coast news production capability. In January 1989, "Marketplace" premiered on 70 affiliates. After an initial struggle for acceptance and financial support, the program was carried daily by approximately 200 stations with 2 million weekly listeners at the end of four years, and had attracted a prestigious group of underwriters led by General Electric.

"Marketplace" is produced by KUSC-FM at the University of Southern California, not by APR, although the arrangements surrounding APR's initial investment and continuing support of the program resemble a co-production or co-ownership situation. Furthermore, "Marketplace" producers have built a system of 10 domestic bureaus based at public radio stations, overseas bureaus in London and Tokyo and cooperative relationships with organizations such as the *Economist* newspaper, which supplies two segments weekly. In innovative ways such as these, APR has become more actively engaged in program development while continuing to stand clear of day-to-day editorial and production management.

In recent years, NPR also has broadened its approach to program production, particularly in the domain of non-news programming. In seeking to rebuild a competitive presence in cultural programming, it might be said that NPR borrowed a page from the APR playbook, acquiring a local station production, "Car Talk," which has become a centerpiece of its cultural programming bundle. NPR also has begun vying with APR to acquire cultural and performance specials and limited series, previously APR's field largely by default. One hopes that the result will be a more robust marketplace for stations and independent producers in the years ahead, yielding greater incentives for talented producers to work in radio.

With the changes in public radio over the past decade, it seems clear that the two major suppliers of national programming are operating on an ever more level playing field, and that their market shares are converging. NPR supplied 20 percent of public radio programming in 1987, 21 percent in 1991; APR supplied 9 percent of station schedules in 1987, up to 13 percent in 1991.

Further, although both APR and NPR are growing, neither's growth is occurring at the expense of the other. Rather, the largest shift in programming patterns over the past five years appears to be that stations are using more nationally produced and distributed programming. In 1987, station schedules were 60 percent locally produced programs and 40 percent national shows. By 1991, the ratio was 54 percent local, 46 percent national, meaning that an all-day station was consuming some 525 hours more national programming a year.

There are at least two explanations for this trend, which may well be ongoing. First, with the addition of new public stations and the upgrading of existing ones, major urban areas increasingly are served by more than a single public radio signal. With multiple channel options available to listeners, more stations are focusing on a single "format" (e.g., news or classical music) to achieve the clearest possible identity amidst a sea of choices. As digital technology comes to radio later in the decade, an even wider range of options will open up for listeners, and public stations will need to field the highest quality schedule possible, which is likely to mean a focused blend of national and local programming.

Second, the development of a national program marketplace offering more than 30,000 hours a year of series and specials for public radio means that there is sufficient material available to program first-class news, classical music, jazz or contemporary music stations with little or no redundancy, an option not available a decade ago. APR alone distributed more than 18,000 hours of programming in 1992, roughly half music and cultural, half news and information, including a full 24-hours daily of the BBC World Service.

What emerges from this still-unfolding story is a portrait of public radio considerably at odds with the widely shared image of a system dominated by one national producer-distributor supplying a homogeneous network of stations. In fact, the public radio reality is much more diverse and arguably a great deal richer.

SOURCES OF PUBLIC RADIO PROGRAMMING, 1991

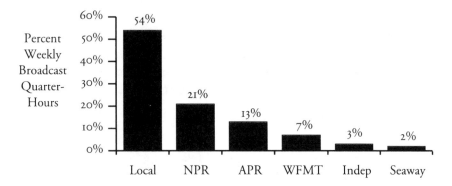

Competition within public radio is generating energy and imagination about how to meet the changing needs of stations and listeners. A recent independent survey confirmed that most station managers believe the presence of a second national network makes all producers and distributors more responsive to their needs, which also helps hold costs in line.

Whether the resources can be found to extend public radio's appeal to more Americans and to develop a next generation of talents like Garrison Keillor and Cokie Roberts remains to be seen. But 10 years from now, it seems likely that competition will have propelled public radio forward, not held it back. And what could be more thoroughly American than that?

Stephen L. Salyer is president of Public Radio International (formerly American Public Radio).

V
Books

22

"Seems Radio Is Here to Stay"

Mary Ann Watson

The Golden Web
Erik Barnouw (Oxford University Press, 1968)

Empire of the Air: The Men Who Made Radio
Tom Lewis (HarperPerennial, 1991)

Radio Comedy
Arthur Frank Wertheim (Oxford University Press, 1979)

Norman Corwin and Radio: The Golden Years
R. LeRoy Bannerman (The University of Alabama Press, 1986)

The Portable Radio in American Life
Michael B. Schiffer (The University of Arizona Press, 1991)

Radio in the Television Age
Peter Fornatale and Joshua E. Mills (Overlook Press, 1980)

The Radio Station
Michael C. Keith and Joseph M. Krause (Focal Press, 1993)

In 1939, at the behest of the National Association of Broadcasters, CBS aired a program called "Seems Radio Is Here to Stay," part of an industrywide public relations campaign to raise consciousness of radio and to heighten listeners' esteem for the medium that had become so central to American life.

The timing was propitious, coming just as network radio was poised to reach its zenith. By 1939, through the hard years of the Depression, it

195

had become a reassuring presence, a dependable companion and friend. But, as with all things constant and steady, radio's beneficiaries were growing complacent. The NAB wanted to give the audience a gentle tap on the shoulder.

The assignment to script, produce and direct CBS's contribution to the evangelical mission went to the network's *wunderkind*, 28-year-old Norman Corwin. The homey title selected for his show belied the poignant poetry it contained:

"We wish a thousand words with you concerning magics that would make a Merlin turn pistachio with envy: The miracle, worn ordinary now, of just such business as this between your ears and us, and ocean tides of ether," Corwin's script ran.

"Do you grant radio is here to stay? Then grant this further: That the mystic ethers were established well before the first word passed between two men. It's only latterly we've seen that speech is buoyant in these waves: a puff or two of years, that's all it is. There may this very moment be, as close to us as one discoverer away, whole firmaments of stuffs awaiting comprehension...."

Poignant in retrospect, with television only a puff or two of years away, Corwin's script caught the mystical nature of the medium. As listeners contemplated his words, the trauma of world war approached— as did radio's most glorious and romantic era.

Two dramatic chapters of American history in this century—the Great Depression and World War II—share radio as a key player. And no storyteller documents the medium more elegantly than Erik Barnouw. His landmark work is the starting point in understanding the evolution of our mass culture.

In 1959, after the London office of Oxford University Press commissioned Asa Briggs to write a three-volume history of British broadcasting, Barnouw, a professor of dramatic arts in the film division at Columbia University, received a call from Oxford's New York office. Untrained as a historian, Barnouw was surprised to be invited to produce a similar three-part history of American broadcasting. It is our good fortune that Barnouw did not shun such a daunting project, and even better fortune that novelists—not academic authors—provided his stylistic inspiration and models.

The collection, *A History of Broadcasting in the United States* (known by all students of mass media simply as "The Trilogy"), includes *A Tower* in *Babel*, which traces radio to 1933, *The Golden Web* (1933–1953) and *The Image Empire* (1953-1970). A condensation of the three volumes, *Tube of Plenty*, carries broadcasting's story through the monumental changes of the 1980s, but Oxford wisely continues to publish the original editions.

Though Barnouw was not the first author to chronicle the rise of broadcasting, his work was ground breaking. Making extensive use of primary source materials and oral histories, he inspired a generation of scholars to study media not for its own sake, but for its social impact. Almost single-handedly, Erik Barnouw legitimized broadcasting as a field of serious scholarly inquiry.

The Golden Web offers the full sweep of network radio's heyday. It's a long mural that Barnouw paints, with a multitude of elements—technology, economics, regulation, programming and audience effects. Beyond its scope, *The Golden Web* is also a compelling read because there are heroes and villains along the way. A reviewer once wrote that Barnouw's narrative technique "makes us feel contempt for those who abuse power and kinship with those oppressed."

Two abusers of radio's power in the 1930s were Father Charles Coughlin, a Michigan parish priest, and Huey Long, who became Louisiana's U.S. senator in 1933 after serving four years as governor. Barnouw yokes the demagogic pair and explains their attempts to influence listeners by fanning passions and prejudices. Coughlin's attacks on international bankers grew into anti-Semitism and pro-Nazism, hatred that seemed sanctioned by the church. Long's quest for dictatorial control of his state exploited economic fears by promising that shared national wealth would provide guaranteed annual incomes, limited work hours and old-age pensions.

Although, of course, these electronic "pied pipers" did not prevail (Long was assassinated in 1935 and Coughlin was eventually forced off the air by his clerical superiors), there is a timeless lesson in their stories that Barnouw subtly conveys. The emancipating potential of the electronic age can easily be twisted by those who appeal to the most base instincts in human nature. A present-day reader of *The Golden Web* can't help but be reminded of the recent controversy over shock-jock Howard Stern's radio show and his exploitation of hate-mongering as a vehicle for laughs.

Another figure in radio history whom Barnouw introduces is a champion of the oppressed. In the summer of 1943, while soldiers black and white were fighting a common enemy, a race riot erupted on the streets of Detroit, leaving 34 dead and 700 injured. Dramatist William Robson, after studying available police reports and interviewing witnesses, wrote the play *Open Letter on Race Hatred*. Despite the refusal of several Southern affiliates to carry the program, CBS stood by its commitment to air it.

That dramatization of the racial misunderstandings that fueled the Detroit violence closed with a postscript by Wendell Willkie, FDR's Republican rival. Willkie had experienced an epiphany about racial matters when he journeyed around the world as a representative of the Roosevelt administration: "Two-thirds of the people who are our allies do not have white skins. And they have long, hurtful memories of the white man's superior attitude in his dealings with them.... One-tenth of the people in this country belong to the Negro race... [and] there are certain things these Negro citizens are entitled to—not as a matter of patronage or tolerance, but as a matter of right."

As Barnouw documents, Robson's 1943 radio drama was a precursor to the advocacy position television would take on the civil rights movement two decades later with impassioned programming like "The American Revolution of '63," which appealed to our better angels. But William Robson paid for his dedication to human rights. Finding himself listed in *Red Channels: The Report on Communist Influence in Radio and Television* in 1950, his livelihood dwindled. Messages of brotherhood between races and countries were suspect in the '50s, and civilizing voices were silenced as network radio's backbone weakened. Erik Barnouw's talent as a social historian is that he not only makes us feel anger about the injustice of the blacklist, but sadness, too, over the senselessness of its damage.

Where Barnouw's scope is panoramic, Tom Lewis cuts a narrower— but deep—swath of history in *Empire of the Air: The Men Who Made Radio*, a saga of scientific discovery replete with personal struggle and corporate conflict.

Through the intertwining stories of three men, Lewis ushers us through the transformation of wireless telegraphy into modern radio broadcasting. The characters are the egotistical Lee De Forest, who discovered, however unwittingly, the audion tube that allowed him to proclaim himself "the father of radio"; the tragic genius Edwin Armstrong, who could not give up a fight despite devastating consequences to his life, and

David Sarnoff, the hard-driving Russian immigrant who became the preening mogul of RCA.

One thread of the tale is the protracted legal battle between De Forest and Armstrong over the patent rights to the regenerative circuit, which was of such importance because it vastly improved the sensitivity of radio receivers. The second part of the plot deals with Armstrong's development of the superior system of FM radio and Sarnoff's profit-driven efforts to hamstring its dissemination to prevent an upheaval of RCA's AM-entrenched empire.

Empire of the Air is a rich, wonderful evocation of how America became "a land of listeners." It also chronicles the end of the era of independent innovators who risked all to support their visions. By mid-century, new technologies were the result of corporate teamwork and military initiatives. No longer would individual pioneers be associated with life-altering invention. How would a "Jeopardy" show contestant respond today if asked for "the Father of the VCR"? "the parent of the compact disc"? "the progenitor of high-definition television"?

Wizardry of another sort is the subject of Arthur Frank Wertheim's *Radio Comedy*, which traces and documents creative genius. In the process, Wertheim reveals much about the American character from the 1920s through the 1950s.

The lion's share of Wertheim's analysis is naturally devoted to comedy programming during the Depression and World War II. The most phenomenally popular radio series of all time, "Amos 'n' Andy," is largely regarded today as a disgraceful part of our heritage, although Wertheim does not dismiss it so glibly. While not excusing negative caricatures of black Americans, he builds a case that "Amos 'n' Andy" was a positive model that helped Americans cope with hardship. References to the Depression on the nightly program were common in the early 1930s and, race aside, the show reflected the problems of countless listeners struggling with unemployment and hunger. The character of Amos Jones, the voice of reason, always provided a reminder that diligence, saving and generosity were basic values that must be preserved. He offered hope that "things is goin' to get better"—"When good times come back again," Amos promised, "people is gonna remember all dis an' know what a rainy day is."

Network radio's function as upholder of the national morale continued through the war years, and it was comedy programming that provided the heaviest artillery. Story lines on shows like "Fibber McGee and Molly," Wertheim relates, "often dealt with such subjects as the draft, sugar rationing, gas and rubber conservation, and the black market." Listeners were urged by the biggest of stars—George Burns and Gracie Allen, Eddie Cantor, Jack Benny, Bob Hope—to help win the war through the purchase of war bonds, contributions to the Red Cross and sacrifice at home.

But a full understanding of radio's place in American life during WWII is impossible without a consideration of the high moments of radio drama in the 1940s. *Norman Corwin and Radio: The Golden Years*, by R. LeRoy Bannerman, helps preserve the record of a short-lived time when network bosses supported gifted artists and provided airtime—without commercial interruption—for programs of genuine quality.

Bannerman's biography of Corwin is more of a valentine to a man and an era than a probing examination, but scholarly detachment is not always feasible when a subject inspires an emotional response. The reader detects that Corwin is Bannerman's hero, well before the last page, though, the reader understands why Corwin is Bannerman's hero.

In the late 1930s, a creative revolution was taking place in American radio. Archibald MacLeish, Orson Welles, Arch Oboler and Irving Reis were among those making waves in an entirely new field of theatrical presentation. But, as Bannerman shows, Corwin conceived and executed his own inimitable radio aesthetic. The "Columbia Workshop" on CBS allowed Corwin, a young man with lambent wit and deep conscience, to experiment with whimsical rhyme and free verse. His reputation as poet of the airwaves blossomed in 1938 with his defiant attack on fascism in "They Fly Through the Air With the Greatest of Ease."

With the U.S. entry into World War II, Corwin's themes of the magnificence of the common man and common woman touched a responsive chord in the American people. Just a week after the attack on Pearl Harbor, "We Hold These Truths"—Corwin's tribute to the 150th anniversary of the Bill of Rights—was broadcast over all four radio networks and reached the largest audience ever assembled for a radio drama. This celebration of freedom stiffened the resolve of a nation being asked to sacrifice so much to preserve it.

Corwin was called upon to create several patriotic radio series during the war years, including a collaboration with Edward R. Murrow on "An American in England." Bannerman details them all. It is the program celebrating Allied victory in Europe, though, that is considered the *tour de force* of Norman Corwin's radio career. "On a Note of Triumph," an epic aural mosaic, is the climax of network radio's golden age.

Rearranging the furniture was a widespread activity in American living rooms in the early 1950s. Stately radio consoles made of finely finished wood were moved aside to make space for a television set—perhaps the Mount Vernon from DuMont, with closing solid wood cabinet doors, or the sleek Raytheon Mayfair. In January 1952, for the first time, more Americans were *watching* their home entertainment in the prime evening hours than were *listening* to it. No longer at the center of the household, radio found new corners to occupy.

The Portable Radio in American Life, an encyclopedic treatment by Michael Brian Schiffer, is a fascinating study of some of those new radio venues that employs an archaeological approach. "Because no item develops in isolation," the author explains in the preface, "the history of everyday objects is a history of the life of a people." Schiffer, the radio archaeologist, examines radio receivers as if they were curious cooking pots or tribal spears, placing them in the context of a culture that needed radios for its existence.

Portable tube radios, once a luxury reserved for the wealthy, became a common middle-class acquisition by the dawn of the '50s. Plastic sets in the size and shape of a lunch box came in an assortment of colors—housewives could match the kitchen wallpaper with a set in Caribbean blue, and Swedish red might go nicely with the slipcovers in the rec room.

Radio was adapting to its post-war fate. Big-budget network shows that appealed to the whole family gave way to local disc jockey programs catering to specialized audiences. Teen-agers had already been targeted as an attractive market segment when the "revolution in miniature" elevated beboppers to the cynosure of the industry's affection. The world's first transistor radio, the American-made Regency TR-1, went on sale in 1954, the same year that Bill Haley recorded "Shake, Rattle and Roll." Music that made kids want to dance became what the author calls the "cultural imperative" that transfigured American radio.

Schiffer explains the constellation of factors that allowed Japanese manufacturers to corner the market on the tiny radios that had, by the close of the decade, become the *accoutrement* of teenhood in the USA. Cheap labor, of course, was a primary reason, but other elements came into play as well. For example, miniaturization was more than a novelty to the space-thrifty Japanese—it was serious business, since smaller, lighter radios made for efficient exporting. While many Americans mistook transistor radios for a fad, the Japanese worked diligently to perfect the performance of their "shirt pocket" product. But it was timing, however inadvertent, that was the decisive ingredient that consummated Japanese transistor domination—white teens were getting hep to rhythm and blues.

The story of rock 'n' roll is part and parcel of the history of radio's adaptation to television. In their *Radio in the Television Age,* Peter Fornatale and Joshua E. Mills document the symbiotic relationship between the recording industry and broadcasting. Radio stations needed records to fill airtime cheaply and record companies needed airplay to sell vinyl. The exploits of Alan Freed reveal the interdependence.

Freed, the first major rock 'n' roll DJ, parlayed his power to choose and plug records on WINS-AM in New York to feather his own nest. In exchange for promoting the music of Chuck Berry, Freed negotiated to be listed as co-author on more than a dozen songs, which meant he reaped undeserved royalties every time the records were played. Whatever Alan Freed's ethical lapses, though, he understood the rebelliousness that was at the heart of rock 'n' roll—teen-agers wanted their parents off their backs. Transistor radios helped kids escape into a world of their own, a world they could take with them wherever they went. Earphones simultaneously blocked out and connected.

Other important stories arise in *Radio in the Television Age* as Fornatale and Mills track the genealogy of top-40 formula radio. At midcentury, a scrappy new breed of broadcasters reshaped the medium. Radio promoter Gordon McLendon and programmer Todd Storz were pioneers of format radio built on the solid foundation of localism. Though their legacy is largely neglected, their mark on the character of the medium is deep and enduring. Fornatale and Mills relate a folktale about Todd Storz, for instance, that speaks volumes about his intuitive understanding of contemporary radio programming. Sitting in a bar across the street from his station, he noticed a waitress take some change from her apron pocket and select the same song on the juke box three times in a row. In a flash, Storz realized that human nature favors the familiar—people *wanted* to hear the same songs again and again. So, the number of slots in the jukebox—40—became the length of his station's playlist.

McLendon's innovations in promotion forever changed the nature of radio station competition when he came up with the idea of singsong jingles that repeat station call letters. He milked cash giveaways for every ounce of publicity value. Readers couldn't help but admire his outrageousness. "When McLendon hired disc jockey Johnny Rabbitt at KLIF," the authors noted, "he overturned autos along freeways outside Dallas and had painted on the bottom of each, 'I just flipped for Johnny Rabbit.'"

Fornatale and Mills cover radio through the 1970s, including the flowering of "underground" FM stations that appealed to the emerging counterculture, as well as the formation of National Public Radio. Indeed, it turns out that the creation of NPR, an institution of immeasurable value, was almost an afterthought in the Public Broadcasting Act of 1967. If the two words "or radio" had not been inserted into the legislation before its passage, the bill would have been entirely devoted to television.

The brand-new third edition of a widely used textbook gives a thorough account of how radio came through the 1980s—a time when deregulation made life less complicated for station managers. This unburdening, however, is only a minor relief in the battleground of radio in the 1990s, report Michael C. Keith and Joseph M. Krause in their *The Radio Station*, which details the myriad complexities that test the mettle of those who look to radio for their livelihood.

Formats continue to splinter into finer genres, a process that has been dubbed "frag-out" for audience fragmentation. Even at the height of the British Invasion, who would have seriously predicted an all-Beatles radio station? As the stakes get higher and the margin for error gets smaller, every aspect of station management takes on greater significance. Keith and Krause cover the waterfront for aspiring broadcasters, and for those just curious about how it all works.

The need for research of various types—from audience measurement to a consultant's analysis of a station's sound—is covered in *The Radio Station*, and the nuts and bolts of sales, promotion, newscasts and even engineering are introduced in an accessible way. We gain an appreciation from this comprehensive primer for the enormous collaborative effort expended every day at a radio station.

The remainder of the 1990s promises to be lean years. According to the most recent NAB figures, radio industry revenues dipped 3 percent in 1991 and 59 percent of commercial radio stations in the United States were unprofitable. It's not a business for the timid.

Despite the economic hard times that have rocked the industry, radio—that most malleable and ubiquitous mass medium—is definitely here to stay. There are radios all through most American homes—more than five on average—not just in the living room, but the kitchen, bedroom, basement and bathrooms, plus the Walkman and the one in the car. Most of us listen more than three hours a day. Earth-shattering news first reaches most of us by radio and many of our purchases can be directly linked to the advertising we hear. Talk radio galvanizes public opinion and—like it or not—influences policymakers. Some of us find it easier to disclose a confidence to an anonymous listening audience than to families or friends. Radio helps us decide what to wear in the morning and which route to take to work. Even though radio is integral to the patterns of our lives, we rarely give it a second thought.

Too often radio is treated perfunctorily in college media courses as the obligatory unit that precedes television. But the exploration of radio's dramatic history and its profound contemporary functions is critical to true understanding of how the media have changed what it means to be human.

Men and women born before the advent of broadcasting will still be with us as we greet a new millennium. What remarkable changes they have witnessed in the span of one lifetime! Analysis of the 20th century will be incomplete without full recognition of the way radio changed the world and how we live in it.

The pervasiveness of television, though, has largely eclipsed the scholarly and popular attention radio deserves. In college courses and the pages of local media, television is scrutinized closely while radio receives at best a mention in passing. Radio may be invisible, but it is important to remember that its accomplishments and contributions to our culture are anything but. Maybe another gentle tap on the shoulder is overdue, especially for those who teach, research and write about the electronic media—to overlook radio is to miss the big picture.

Mary Ann Watson is a broadcast historian and associate professor of telecommunication and film at Eastern Michigan University.

For Further Reading

Aitken, Hugh G. J. *The Continuous Wave: Technology and American Radio, 1900–1932*. Princeton, N.J.: Princeton University Press, 1985.

____. *Syntony and Spark: The Origins of Radio*. Princeton, N.J.: Princeton University Press, 1985.

Bannerman, R. LeRoy. *Norman Corwin and Radio: The Golden Years*. Tuscaloosa, Ala.: University of Alabama Press, 1986.

Barnouw, Erik. *The Sponsor*. New York: Oxford University Press, 1978.

____. *The Image Empire: A History of Broadcasting in the United States Since 1953*. New York: Oxford University Press, 1970.

____. *The Golden Web: A History of Broadcasting in the United States, 1933–1953*. New York: Oxford University Press, 1968.

____. *A Tower in Babel: A History of Broadcasting in the United States to 1933*. New York: Oxford University Press, 1966.

Bilby, Kenneth. *The General: David Sarnoff and the Rise of the Communications Industry*. New York: Harper and Row, 1986.

Briggs, Asa. *The BBC: The First 50 Years*. London: Oxford University Press, 1985.

Broadcasting, editors of. *The First 50 Years of Broadcasting*. Washington, D.C.: Broadcasting Publications, 1982.

____. *Broadcasting & Cable Yearbook 1993*. Washington, D.C.: Broadcasting/Bowker, 1993. (annual, 2 vols.)

Cantril, Hadley, and Gordon W. Allport. *The Psychology of Radio*. New York: Harper & Bros., 1935. (Reprinted by Arno Press, 1971.)

Chester, Edward C. *Radio, Television and American Politics*. New York: Sheed and Ward, 1969.

Chorba, Frank, ed. *Journal of Radio Studies*. Topeka, Kan.: Washburn University. (annual)

The Communications Act. Washington, D.C.: U.S. Government Printing Office, regularly updated.

De Forest, Lee. *Father of Radio*. Chicago: Wilcox & Follett, 1950.

Delong, Thomas A. *The Mighty Music Box: The Golden Age of Musical Radio*. Los Angeles: Amber Crest Books, 1980.

Douglas, Susan J. *Inventing American Broadcasting, 1899–1922*. Baltimore, Md.: Johns Hopkins University Press, 1987.

Dreher, Carl. *Sarnoff: An American Success.* New York: Quadrangle/New York Times Books, 1977.

Duncan, James. *American Radio.* Indianapolis: Duncan Media Enterprises, bi-monthly.

Dunning, John. *Tune in Yesterday: The Ultimate Encyclopedia of Old-Time Radio, 1925–1976.* Englewood Cliffs, N.J.: Prentice Hall, 1976.

Eberly, Philip K. *Music in the Air: America's Changing Tastes in Popular Music, 1920–1980.* New York: Hastings House, 1982.

Fornatale, Peter, and Joshua E. Mills. *Radio in the Television Age.* Woodstock, N.Y.: Overlook Press, 1980.

Greenfield, Thomas Allen. *Radio: A Reference Guide.* Westport, Conn.: Greenwood, 1989.

Harmon, Jim. *The Great Radio Heroes.* New York: Doubleday, 1967.

____. *The Great Radio Comedians.* New York: Doubleday, 1970.

Head, Sydney W., Christopher H. Sterling and Lemuel B. Schofield. *Broadcasting in America: A Survey of Electronic Media.* Boston: Houghton-Mifflin, 1994 (7th ed.).

Henderson, Amy. *On the Air: Pioneers of American Broadcasting.* Washington, D.C.: Smithsonian Institution Press, 1988.

Hijiya, James A. *Lee De Forest and the Fatherhood of Radio.* Cranberry, N.J.:Lehigh Unversity Press, 1992.

Hilliard, Robert L., and Michael C. Keith. *The Broadcast Century: A Biography of American Broadcasting.* Stoneham, Mass.: Focal Press, 1992.

Inglis, Andrew F. *Behind the Tube.* Stoneham, Mass.: Focal Press, 1990.

Kahn, Douglas, and Gregory Whitehead, eds. *Wireless Imagination: Sound, Radio and the Avant-Garde.* Cambridge, Mass.: MIT Press, 1992.

Keillor, Garrison. *WLT: A Radio Romance.* New York: Penguin Books, 1991.

Keith, Michael C. *Radio Programming: Consultancy and Formatics.* Stoneham, Mass.: Focal Press, 1987.

Keith, Michael C., and Joseph M. Krause. *The Radio Station.* Boston: Focal Press, 1993 (3rd ed.).

Landry, Robert J. *This Fascinating Radio Business.* Indianapolis: Bobbs-Merrill, 1946.

Lazarsfeld, Paul F., and P.L. Kendall. *Radio Listening in America.* Englewood Cliffs, N.J.: Prentice Hall, 1948.

Lessing, Lawrence. *Man of High Fidelity.* New York: Lippincott, 1956. (rev. ed. with new foreword. Bantam, 1969.)

Levin, Murray B. *Talk Radio and the American Dream.* Lexington, Mass.: Lexington Books, 1987.

Lewis, Peter M., and Jerry Booth. *The Invisible Medium: Public, Commercial and Community Radio.* Washington, D.C.: Howard University Press, 1990.

Lewis, Tom. *Empire of the Air: The Men Who Made Radio.* New York: Harper Collins, 1991.

Lichty, Lawrence W., and Malachi C. Topping. *A Source Book on the History of Radio.* New York: Hasting House, 1975.

M Street Journal. New York: M Street Corp., weekly.

MacDonald, J. Fred. *Don't Touch That Dial: Radio Programming in American Life, 1920–1960.* Chicago: Nelson-Hall, 1979.

MacFarland, David T. *Contemporary Radio Programming Strategies.* Hillsdale, N.J.: Erlbaum, 1990.

National Association of Broadcasters. *NAB Legal Guide to Broadcast Law.* Washington, D.C.: National Association of Broadcasters, 1988 (3rd ed.).

Radio & Records. Los Angeles: Radio & Records Inc., weekly.

Radio Ink, Boynton Beach, Fla., monthly.

The Radio Industry: The Story of Its Development. Chicago and New York: A.W. Shaw, 1928. (reprinted by Arno Press, 1971.)

Radio Marketing Guide and Fact Book for Advertisers. New York: Radio Advertising Bureau, 1993. (Annual).

Schiffer, Michael Brian. *The Portable Radio in American Life.* Tucson, Ariz.: University of Arizona Press, 1991.

Settel, Irving. *A Pictorial History of Radio.* New York: Crown, 1967 (2nd ed.)

Shanes, Ed. *Cutting Through: Strategies and Tactics of Radio.* Houston: Shane Media, 1990.

Siepmann, Charles M. *Radio's Second Chance.* Boston: Atlantic, Little Brown, 1946.

Smith, Wes. *The Pied Pipers of Rock 'n' Roll: Radio Deejays of the '50s and '60s.* Marietta, Ga.: Longstreet Press, 1989.

Soley, Lawrence C. *Radio Warfare.* New York: Praeger, 1989.

Soley, Lawrence C., and John S. Nichols. *Clandestine Radio Broadcasting: A Study of Revolutionary and Counterrevolutionary Electronic Communication.* New York: Praeger, 1987.

Sterling, Christopher H., and John M. Kittross. *Stay Tuned: A Concise History of American Broadcasting.* Belmont, Calif.: Wadsworth, 1990 (2nd ed.).

Wertheim, Arthur Frank. *Radio Comedy.* New York: Oxford University Press, 1979.

Wood, James. *History of International Broadcasting.* Piscataway, N.J.: IEEE Publications, 1992.

Index